Censorship

OPPOSING VIEWPOINTS®

Other Books of Related Interest

Censorship

OPPOSING VIEWPOINTS®

Tamara L. Roleff, *Book Editor*

Bonnie Szumski, *Editorial Director*
Scott Barbour, *Managing Editor*

OPPOSING
VIEWPOINTS®
SERIES

Greenhaven Press, Inc., San Diego, California

Cover photo: © Linda Mae Tratechaud Design

Library of Congress Cataloging-in-Publication Data

Censorship : opposing viewpoints / Tamara L. Roleff, book editor.
    p. cm. — (Opposing viewpoints series)
    Includes bibliographical references and index.
    ISBN 1-56510-957-0 (lib. bdg. : alk. paper) —
ISBN 1-56510-956-2 (pbk. : alk. paper)
    1. Censorship—United States. I. Roleff, Tamara L., 1959–
II. Opposing viewpoints series (Unnumbered)

Z658.U5 C43 2002
363.3'1—dc21   2001016037
                                                  CIP

Every effort has been made to trace the owners of copyrighted material.

Greenhaven Press, Inc., P.O. Box 289009
San Diego, CA 92198-9009

"Congress shall make
no law. . . abridging the
freedom of speech, or of
the press."

First Amendment to the U.S. Constitution

The basic foundation of our democracy is the First
Amendment guarantee of freedom of expression.
The Opposing Viewpoints Series is dedicated to the
concept of this basic freedom and the idea that it is
more important to practice it than to enshrine it.

Contents

Why Consider Opposing Viewpoints?

"The only way in which a human being can make some approach to knowing the whole of a subject is by hearing what can be said about it by persons of every variety of opinion and studying all modes in which it can be looked at by every character of mind. No wise man ever acquired his wisdom in any mode but this."

John Stuart Mill

In our media-intensive culture it is not difficult to find differing opinions. Thousands of newspapers and magazines and dozens of radio and television talk shows resound with differing points of view. The difficulty lies in deciding which opinion to agree with and which "experts" seem the most credible. The more inundated we become with differing opinions and claims, the more essential it is to hone critical reading and thinking skills to evaluate these ideas. Opposing Viewpoints books address this problem directly by presenting stimulating debates that can be used to enhance and teach these skills. The varied opinions contained in each book examine many different aspects of a single issue. While examining these conveniently edited opposing views, readers can develop critical thinking skills such as the ability to compare and contrast authors' credibility, facts, argumentation styles, use of persuasive techniques, and other stylistic tools. In short, the Opposing Viewpoints Series is an ideal way to attain the higher-level thinking and reading skills so essential in a culture of diverse and contradictory opinions.

In addition to providing a tool for critical thinking, Opposing Viewpoints books challenge readers to question their own strongly held opinions and assumptions. Most people form their opinions on the basis of upbringing, peer pressure, and personal, cultural, or professional bias. By reading carefully balanced opposing views, readers must directly confront new ideas as well as the opinions of those with whom they disagree. This is not to simplistically argue that everyone who reads opposing views will—or should—change his or her opinion. Instead, the series enhances readers' understanding of their own views by encouraging confrontation with opposing ideas. Careful examination of others' views can lead to the readers' understanding of the logical inconsistencies in their own opinions, perspective on why they hold an opinion, and the consideration of the possibility that their opinion requires further evaluation.

Evaluating Other Opinions

To ensure that this type of examination occurs, Opposing Viewpoints books present all types of opinions. Prominent spokespeople on different sides of each issue as well as well-known professionals from many disciplines challenge the reader. An additional goal of the series is to provide a forum for other, less known, or even unpopular viewpoints. The opinion of an ordinary person who has had to make the decision to cut off life support from a terminally ill relative, for example, may be just as valuable and provide just as much insight as a medical ethicist's professional opinion. The editors have two additional purposes in including these less known views. One, the editors encourage readers to respect others' opinions—even when not enhanced by professional credibility. It is only by reading or listening to and objectively evaluating others' ideas that one can determine whether they are worthy of consideration. Two, the inclusion of such viewpoints encourages the important critical thinking skill of objectively evaluating an author's credentials and bias. This evaluation will illuminate an author's reasons for taking a particular stance on an issue and will aid in readers' evaluation of the author's ideas.

It is our hope that these books will give readers a deeper understanding of the issues debated and an appreciation of the complexity of even seemingly simple issues when good and honest people disagree. This awareness is particularly important in a democratic society such as ours in which people enter into public debate to determine the common good. Those with whom one disagrees should not be regarded as enemies but rather as people whose views deserve careful examination and may shed light on one's own.

Thomas Jefferson once said that "difference of opinion leads to inquiry, and inquiry to truth." Jefferson, a broadly educated man, argued that "if a nation expects to be ignorant and free . . . it expects what never was and never will be." As individuals and as a nation, it is imperative that we consider the opinions of others and examine them with skill and discernment. The Opposing Viewpoints Series is intended to help readers achieve this goal.

David L. Bender and Bruno Leone,
Founders

Greenhaven Press anthologies primarily consist of previously published material taken from a variety of sources, including periodicals, books, scholarly journals, newspapers, government documents, and position papers from private and public organizations. These original sources are often edited for length and to ensure their accessibility for a young adult audience. The anthology editors also change the original titles of these works in order to clearly present the main thesis of each viewpoint and to explicitly indicate the opinion presented in the viewpoint. These alterations are made in consideration of both the reading and comprehension levels of a young adult audience. Every effort is made to ensure that Greenhaven Press accurately reflects the original intent of the authors included in this anthology.

Introduction

"One man's hate speech is another man's political statement."

Charles Levendosky, Liberal Opinion Weekly,
August 17, 1998

Benjamin Smith, a twenty-one-year-old member of the racist group World Church of the Creator, went on a hate-filled, three-day shooting rampage over the Fourth of July weekend in 1999 in which he killed two and wounded nine—all minorities. He began the weekend by shooting at a group of Jews who were leaving their synagogue in Chicago, Illinois, wounding six of them. An hour later, he was driving down a residential street in Skokie, where Ricky Byrdsong, a black former basketball coach at Northwestern University in Evanston, was jogging with two of his children. Smith shot and killed Byrdsong, forty-three, with seven bullets to the back. The next day, Smith shot at a group of Asians near the University of Illinois. On the last day of his shooting spree, Smith killed Won-Joon Yoon, a twenty-six-year-old Korean-American as he left church in Bloomington. Smith then stole a van and led police on a chase before killing himself with a gunshot to his head.

Many people argue that the racist speech of the World Church of the Creator and other hate groups—especially on the Internet—encourages white supremacists like Smith to act on their beliefs and commit hate crimes. In fact, Sherialynn Byrdsong believes the presence of hate groups on the Internet is directly responsible for her husband's murder. The Internet has become a popular tool for racist groups to promote their message of white supremacy and to recruit new members. The number of hate sites on the Internet has grown from one in 1995 to over twenty-eight hundred in 2000, according to the Simon Wiesenthal Center, an organization that monitors anti-Semitism and hate crimes. Children and teens are especially attracted to Internet hate sites because they can satisfy their curiosity about white supremacy in private and meet others online who share their racist views. Some hate groups have incorporated games and graphics into their web pages designed to specifically appeal to younger viewers.

Because hate can be dangerous, as Smith's victims and their families are well aware, and because children and teens are attracted to hate groups' websites, some people, including Sherialynn Byrdsong, want to ban hate sites on the Internet. Critics believe online hate is much more powerful than other kinds of racist propaganda because it is available and easily accessible twenty-four hours a day. According to Sherialynn Byrdsong,

> Ben Smith was probably greatly influenced by things that he heard and saw over the Internet, because there seems to be a lot of sites where people can visit to learn about hate and hate groups, white supremacist movements, and philosophies. I believe he became so brainwashed . . . that what he was learning overpowered any kind of human esteem for the lives of people who were different from himself.

Those who support censorship of online hate know that the Constitution permits censorship of some speech. The Court has ruled that obscenity and "fighting words" are two exceptions to the First Amendment's protection of free speech. Byrdsong argues that an exception should be made for hate speech as well: "I doubt seriously if the writers of our Constitution and Bill of Rights intended that freedom of speech could be a way that people can spread their hate philosophy. I don't think that free speech means hate speech."

Others disagree, however, contending that the right to free speech must include hate speech. Eric Zorn, a columnist with the *Chicago Tribune*, argues, "The concept of freedom of speech means nothing— less than nothing—if it doesn't extend to the speech of those with whom you have profound disagreements. . . . They're the ones who need it."

Hate groups, like many of the political and social protesters of the second half of the twentieth century, depend on being provocative and inflammatory simply to get people's attention. The protests over the Vietnam War, civil rights, women's rights, and abortion were very unpopular at their inception (and some continue to be). Critics of censorship claim that once restrictions are placed on hate speech, they may then be placed on other unpopular forms of speech. According to Charles Levendosky, a noted commentator on First Amendment issues, "socio-political movements could be crushed before they even started." Therefore, he asserts, hate speech, despite how despicable it may be, should not be censored. "One man's hate speech is another man's political statement. And political commentary has—and should have—the highest First Amendment protection."

Besides being politically unfeasible, some critics maintain that trying to censor hate speech on the Internet would actually benefit the hate groups. Syndicated columnist Scott Rosenberg explains how such a plan would backfire against the censors:

> Shutting down Web sites that publish idiotic racist and anti-Semitic ideas might give people a sense of having struck a blow for sanity. But it's not very practical. Close down one Web site and another five spring up. And it tends to backfire, giving racists a chance to pose as martyrs in the cause of free speech.

Rosenberg also points out that people will not become converts to white supremacy simply by being exposed to hate speech. In the "marketplace of ideas," first proposed by philosopher John Stuart Mill, ideas—both good and bad—are set out before the public, who can then "vigorously and earnestly" debate them. Stuart and his followers contend that when ideas are examined in a free and open forum—one without censorship—the good ideas (such as tolerance) survive, while the bad ideas (such as racism and white supremacy) disappear.

The controversy over hate speech—whether spoken, written, or transmitted through cyberspace—is similar to other debates about censorship. Pornography and its accessibility online, violent and sexually explicit movies and music, offensive art—all have their critics who argue for censorship. These topics and others are some of the issues discussed in *Censorship: Opposing Viewpoints*, which contains the following chapters: Should the Right to Free Speech Be Restricted? Should Pornography Be Censored? Should Schools and Libraries Practice Censorship? Should the Arts and Entertainment Industries Be Censored? As long as people find some speech and art offensive, the question will remain whether some speech should be exempt from the protection guaranteed by the First Amendment.

CHAPTER 1

Should the Right to Free Speech Be Restricted?

Chapter Preface

A survey of attitudes toward the First Amendment conducted in early 2000 shows how conflicted Americans are toward the right to free speech. The First Amendment Center, an organization that works to protect freedom of expression, found in a poll of 1,015 adults that while a majority of Americans accept the ideal of freedom of speech in theory, they are less likely to accept free speech in reality. The survey found that many Americans favor restrictions on speech, especially on speech that is offensive to some groups.

According to the survey, 67 percent of those polled believe remarks offensive to racial groups should be prohibited, and 53 percent believe offensive speech directed at religious groups should be banned. In addition, a slight majority of 51 percent thinks that offensive art should not be shown in a public place. Another 74 percent would prohibit people from being able to burn the American flag as a form of protest. A significant number—31 percent—said a group should not be allowed to hold a rally for an unpopular or offensive cause. And yet, the Supreme Court has ruled that all of these restrictions are unconstitutional.

According to Paul McMasters of the Freedom Forum, an organization affiliated with the First Amendment Center, "Americans truly believe they believe in free speech," but when confronted with "the speech of the radical, the rascal, even the revolting—we become unsure." The authors in the following chapter examine some of the issues that provoke Americans' ambivalence toward restrictions on their First Amendment guarantee of free speech.

| *"Judicious government censorship is not the enemy of freedom but its guarantor."*

Government Censorship Would Benefit Society

Roger Kimball

Constant exposure to graphic sex and violence in the entertainment media brutalizes and desensitizes the viewer, argues Roger Kimball in the following viewpoint. Society was better off when the government censored sex and violence, as it did throughout most of American history. Kimball maintains that when graphic depictions of sex are forbidden, the audience's imagination makes the story richer. Kimball is the managing editor of *New Criterion* and author of *The Long March: How the Cultural Revolution of the 1960s Changed America*.

As you read, consider the following questions:
1. According to the author, why is the claim that parents should censor their children's films false?
2. What is the one thing Sigmund Freud was right about, in Kimball's opinion?
3. What two reason does Kimball give to support government censorship?

Reprinted from "The Case for Censorship," by Roger Kimball, *The Wall Street Journal*, October 8, 2000, by permission of the author and *The Wall Street Journal*. Copyright © 2000 Dow Jones and Company, Inc. All rights reserved.

Isn't it time someone put in a good word for censorship? After pocketing his loot from the nice people in Hollywood, Sen. Joseph Lieberman assured them that "we will never, never put the government in the position of telling you by law, through law, what to make. We will noodge* you, but we will never become censors."

Why not? As William Bennett pointed out, Sen. Lieberman sang a very different tune before he became Al Gore's running mate. He thundered against the "culture of carnage," and warned that if Hollywood continued "to market death and degradation to our children . . . then one way or another, the government will act."

What's wrong with a little censorship? Until quite recently, all sorts of things were censored in American society. There were very strict rules about what you could show on television and in movies, what you could describe in books and what you could reproduce in magazines. Were we worse off then?

Think about it. Not so long ago, you could turn on the television and be absolutely certain that you weren't going to be confronted with potty-mouthed people taking off their clothes. You could go down to the local newsstand and not see rows of pornography for sale. You could go to the movies and not worry about witnessing someone's viscera splashed across the screen. You could see commercials for Chesterfields on television, but the ads on buses were clearly distinguishable from pedophiliac fantasy. Was that a repressive time?

In some ways, yes. But is that sort of repression a bad thing? In my opinion, Sigmund Freud was wrong about almost everything. Yet he was right when he observed that civilization is founded on one very short word: *No.* Without what Freud called sublimation, you don't get civilization. Edmund Burke made a similar point: "Men are qualified for civil liberty," he said, "in exact proportion to their disposition to put moral chains on their own appetites. . . . Society cannot exist unless a controlling power upon will and appetite be placed somewhere, and the less of it there is within, the more there is without."

*Editor's note: Noodge is a Yiddish term for a gentle nag.

Just the other day, the *New York Times* ran a front-page story with the headline "Parents Say Censoring Films Is Their Job Not Politicians'." What rot! Parents can do absolutely nothing to censor the entertainment industry. And it is clear that the entertainment industry is not going to censor itself. As always, the people who run it will go exactly as far as the law allows them to go. In my opinion, the law currently allows them to go much too far.

Does that mean I am in favor of—gasp—government censorship? Sure. Would it be such a bad thing if pornography were a little harder to come by, if "gross-out" movies were a little less gross, if there were less violence on television? Believe me, the republic would survive.

And the right of free speech? Well, what about it? Recent court cases notwithstanding, the First Amendment was not framed in order to protect pornography or depictions of violence. Indeed, until the 1950s, the courts explicitly excluded free speech as a defense for trafficking in obscene materials. Are we better off now?

Censorship Is the Only Answer

The mass media—movies, television and recordings—need to be regulated, and not only because of appeals to irresponsible lust. They have immersed us in violence as well, habituated us to the most extreme brutality, held it up as a model and surrounded us by images of hateful human types so memorable as to cause a psychological insecurity that is dangerous. The only answer is governmental regulation, if necessary prior to publication—that is, censorship.

David Lowenthal, *Weekly Standard*, August 23, 1999.

Even if one is an absolutist when it comes to the First Amendment, it is worth noting that the existence of a right to do something does not mean that it is a morally or socially acceptable thing to do. As John Searle, the philosopher, has observed, "any healthy human institution—family, state, university, ski team—grants its members rights that far exceed the bounds of morally acceptable behavior.... The gulf between the rights granted and the performance expected is bridged by the responsibility of the members." When that responsibility falters, society requires moral strictures and legal penalties to make up the difference.

It is also worth noting that many people who consider themselves First Amendment absolutists have no problem with the censorship that comes with political correctness. When you can lose your job and be subject to legal penalties because you tell a joke around the office water cooler, you are living in a very censorious society. Maybe we need a little less political correctness and a little more moral restraint.

In any event, there are plenty of reasons to support government censorship when it comes to depictions of sex and violence. For one thing, it would encourage the entertainment industry to turn out material that is richer erotically. This may seem paradoxical. But one problem with the almost-anything-goes attitude we have now is that it can make for boring and simplistic fare.

There is, if I remember correctly, only one kiss in Henry James's *The Golden Bowl*. But that novel communicates a deeper and more fully human eroticism than a book full of dirty words and the deeds they name.

It's the same in the movies. It is fashionable today to decry the old Hollywood code that proscribed showing even a married couple together in a double bed. But what a goad to imagination and cleverness that code turned out to be! Anyone who has seen Clark Gable and Claudette Colbert in *It Happened One Night*, or Myrna Loy and William Powell together in anything, knows that you do not need nudity or graphic language to make a sexy movie. On the contrary, if those movies had included what are euphemistically referred to as "adult situations," their charm, including their erotic charm, would have been killed.

Another reason to support government censorship is that it would help temper the extraordinary brutality of popular culture. Perhaps you have seen "studies" by some experts telling you that depictions of violence do not lead to violent behavior. Pay them no heed. Even if true, which I doubt, there can be no question that brutality brutalizes. It corrupts taste and poisons the imagination.

Society has an interest in protecting free speech and the free circulation of ideas. It also has an interest in protecting the moral sensibility of its citizens, especially the young. Freedom without morality degenerates into the servitude of libertinage. Which is why judicious government censorship is not the enemy of freedom but its guarantor.

> *"The urge to censor and sanitize public discourse and entertainment comes of fear—fear of youth, fear of new technology, fear of tastes and values that don't match their own."*

Speech Should Not Be Restricted

Paul McMasters

Many people argue that society will fall into ruin unless the government steps in to restrict Americans' exposure to sex and violence. Paul McMasters contends, however, that restrictions proposed by the "speech police" are actually censorship and are unnecessary. He maintains that Americans are quite capable of reading and watching what they choose without becoming immoral or criminal. McMasters is the First Amendment ombudsman for the Freedom Forum, an international organization that works to protect free speech.

As you read, consider the following questions:
1. What is David Lowenthal's prophecy for America, as cited by McMasters?
2. Who is Thomas Bowdler, and what is his legacy?
3. According to the author, what is behind the urge to censor?

Reprinted, with permission, from "Speech Police—on the Left and Right—Trample Freedom of Expression in the Name of Virtue," by Paul McMasters, *The Freedom Forum Online*, September 8, 1999, found at http://199.183.110.96/first/1999/9/8ombudsman.asp.

D avid Lowenthal, professor emeritus of political science at Boston College, offered an argument for censorship of the entertainment media in an article recently published in *The Weekly Standard*. Lowenthal is inspired by two convictions: That Hollywood is dishing out too much sex and violence and that we consumers like it too much for our own good.

In a rather remarkable statement to find in one of the nation's leading conservative publications, Lowenthal wrote, "Government, and government alone, has a chance of blocking this descent into decadence."

"The choice is clear," he wrote, "either a rigorous censorship of the mass media—or an accelerating descent into barbarism and the destruction, sooner or later, of free society itself."

We must destroy our freedom in order to save it.

Halfhearted Rebuttals

The four distinguished commentators asked to respond to Lowenthal's jeremiad against free speech fumed and fumbled with halfhearted arguments about censorship not being politically practical. They clearly agreed with Lowenthal on one thing: That the Hollywood entertainment industry is the source of most evil in this society.

William Bennett was one of those asked to respond to Lowenthal. Casting himself as a "virtual absolutist on the First Amendment," Bennett endorsed instead the tactics of the "political correctness" movement as a way to sanitize the media to suit his own tastes. "The goal is to turn the people who are polluting our moral environment into social pariahs," Bennett wrote. "Think of what would happen to a political figure, sportscaster, or businessman who uttered ugly racial or ethnic slurs. . . . Our goal should be to see that the same thing happens with entertainment executives."

So instead of government censorship, Bennett proposed governmental coercion. "Congress ought to begin treating the entertainment industry the same way it treats the gun and tobacco industries," he said. In other words, government officials should subject the creators of entertainment to the same sort of inquisitions and treatment as the makers of products that actually kill, sicken and injure people.

It's easy enough for Bennett to take the high road on censorship, of course, since he is not in a position to impose it anyway. But some of his closest allies on this issue—U.S. Sens. Joe Lieberman, John McCain and Sam Brownback, to name a few—do have the power to impose censorship. Clearly, they are in no mood to wait for public opprobrium to kick in.

In fact, they are busy putting the machinery of censorship in place.

Government Attempts at Censorship

[When] Congress returned from the August 1999 recess, . . . high on the agenda for Brownback [was] the creation of a special committee to scrutinize American culture in general and the entertainment media in particular. "We just need to ask where our culture has gone and how do you bring it back to where we all want it," Brownback said.

Meanwhile, Lieberman and McCain are trying to drum up support for the Media Violence Labeling Act of 1999. This bill, ironically proposed as an amendment to the Federal Cigarette Labeling and Advertising Act, would require the development and enforcement of a uniform labeling system for violent content. It would apply to a variety of media, including movies, records, CDs, and video games. The kicker, of course: The law would restrict the sale of any products carrying the labels.

The Federal Trade Commission already is busy subpoenaing mountains of documents from entertainment producers, inquiring into whether the industry violated its own "voluntary" ratings system in its marketing of products.

The U.S. Surgeon General has been ordered to study the impact and influence of violence in the media.

And Sen. Orrin Hatch, chairman of the Senate Judiciary Committee, released a staff report that sums up a complicated and highly qualified body of research by asserting that there is a causal link between violence in the media and violence on the street.

This is a well-worn path to censorship.

Today, the charge down that path is led by the speech police who assail popular culture as the weapon of an "institutional elite" that "wraps themselves in the First Amendment" and are bent on destroying society by entertaining it to death.

This insanity begins as always in a rush to save the populace from the influence of coarse language and entertainment. This is in the best tradition of Thomas Bowdler, the 18th century English editor who cleansed various works of literature of "words and expressions—which cannot with propriety be read aloud in a family." Bowdler managed to make the world a better place by publishing expurgated versions of Shakespeare, Gibbons' history and the Old Testament itself before he wore himself out.

'Shakespeare, ha! That better be the revised, sanitized, approved, nonpornographic edition!'

It's difficult to find any of those safer books these days, but check the dictionary and you will find his most famous legacy, the word "bowdlerized."

The line from Thomas Bowdler to Anthony Comstock spans a century and an ocean, but it is a straight one. Comstock was the New York zealot who convinced himself and others that America was threatened by unpopular social and religious ideas, such as abortion, birth control and gambling.

He boasted of destroying or burning tons of books and periodicals and arresting thousands of people before the nation regained its senses.

Interestingly, campaigns by guardians of our morality to limit and restrict speech always are done in the name of the people. Paradoxically, they do not trust the people to choose for themselves or, having chosen, to think for themselves.

In the minds of the speech police, the rest of us are craven, morally disabled, powerless to resist our worst impulses or the temptations of evil media. We are too uncivilized to understand that censorship is good for us, and we are not to be trusted with an unlabeled video any more than we would be with a lighted cigarette or a loaded gun.

The speech police are everywhere. They traverse the whole political spectrum. The left decries violence in the media. The right laments sex in the media. All sorts of things get caught up in the middle. They justify their zealotry by telling us that there is a higher law than the Constitution and a greater goal than freedom, and that is "virtue."

America Is on the Road to Ruin

There is such a paucity of real ideas about how to solve the ills of our society. So the speech police would have us believe that we cannot be free and virtuous at the same time.

They would have us believe that we are awash in sex and violence.

They would have us believe that reading or viewing violence is tantamount to doing it.

They would have us believe that there is a conspiracy of intellectuals, Hollywood titans, judges and criminals to corrupt our society and lead it into ruin.

And they would have us believe, most remarkably, that the influence of home, family, school and church is no match for the mass media.

A necessary measure of the validity of an idea or movement is the willingness of its proponents to obscure or distort the truth in support of it. The speech police fail that measure.

One wants to believe that those who would save us by censoring us have the best of intentions, but it is difficult. At bottom, the urge to censor and sanitize public discourse and entertainment comes of fear—fear of youth, fear of new technology, fear of tastes and values that don't match their own.

The fact is that there is a richness, diversity and quality in most of today's entertainment that gives the lie to the yelps about filth. The fact is that what comes out of Hollywood simply entertains us; it does not define us. It sure as hell does not make us do bad things to other people.

Instead, we are ordinary Americans who have grown rather fond of the freedom to choose and reject what we read and watch. We believe we are quite capable of doing so without losing either our minds or our morals.

In fact, for more than two centuries now, we have shown ourselves to be quite capable of turning bad words, ideas and images into good lessons.

Censors Will Always Be with Us

Even so, we'll always have the censors with us. Our forebears huddled together in fear, starting and trembling at images and ideas dancing out there in the dark. Rather than bringing those images and ideas into the campfire's glow and confronting them, the tribal guardians shushed the others into silence and hoped that the evil would go away.

Today, the inheritors of that impulse attempt to disembowel the First Amendment in the flickering light of their own fears and misapprehensions.

"[A threat of violence] threatens everyone's free speech. It creates a chilling effect on public discussion when the hate mongers call for killing based on race, national origin, [or] religion."

Hate Speech Should Be Banned

Terrie Albano

Terrie Albano, a member of the national board of the Communist Party, argues in the following viewpoint that the speech of racist hate groups creates an "atmosphere of fear" that stifles free expression. Therefore, he maintains, banning hate speech and the groups that promulgate it would protect the free speech rights of the majority of Americans.

As you read, consider the following questions:
1. According to the author, when were Communists denied their freedom of speech?
2. Which groups does Albano maintain have the right to free speech and which groups do not?
3. How is the class divide over the right to freedom of speech visible, in Albano's view?

Reprinted, with permission, from "On Free Speech and Hate Groups," by Terrie Albano, *People's Weekly World*, August 21, 1999.

Communists are in a unique position to discuss free speech and hate groups. Our unique position comes from our militant history of being in the forefront of free speech fights—from Elizabeth Gurley Flynn as a founder of the ACLU [American Civil Liberties Union] protecting and expanding free speech for workers and their organizations, to fights demanding Paul Robeson [an entertainer and political activist who was blacklisted because of his political beliefs] have the right to speak and perform, to [former Communist Party leader] Gus Hall and the Berkeley Free Speech Movement. Our party has been on the cutting edge of developing and deepening the democratic ideal of free speech by fighting to extend it to the whole working class.

Not All Are Equal

Communists are also in a unique position because Communist Party members were in the most unfortunate and undemocratic position of being denied their freedom of speech. During one of the most undemocratic periods in our country's history, the Cold War McCarthy period, Communists—based on lies, trumped-up charges and witch-hunt hysteria—were victims of the government legally suppressing their freedom of speech. Worse than that, leaders of the Communist Party were jailed for "conspiracy to teach." They were jailed for their beliefs and thoughts!

So when the FBI gets on "Nightline," as it did in the wake of the anti-Semitic and racist shootings and murder in California, and defends the rights of individuals to their beliefs, it is clear that the beliefs of racists and Nazis will be defended by the FBI, but the beliefs of Communists, progressives, trade unionists, peace and civil rights activists will not be.

A Class Divide

Like all things, democracy and free speech have a class basis. There is freedom for the ruling class and corporate interests, whose bottom line is maximum profit and exploitation, and restrictions for the victims of exploitation and those who challenge it.

There may be free speech for bigots, but not free speech for workers trying to organize a union—those workers get fired, black-listed or run out of town.

There may be free speech for Nazis and the Klan, but not free speech for strikers fighting the good fight—the courts hand down anti-picket injunctions preventing strikers from assembling.

Hate Speech Laws Protect Democracy

If protecting hate speech and pornography were essential to safeguarding freedom of inquiry and a flourishing democratic politics, we would expect to find that nations that have adopted hate-speech rules and curbs against pornography would suffer a sharp erosion of the spirit of free inquiry. But this has not happened. A host of Western industrialized nations, including Sweden, Italy, Canada, and Great Britain, have instituted laws against hate speech and hate propaganda, many in order to comply with international treaties and conventions requiring such action. Many of these countries have traditions of respect for free speech at least the equal of ours. No such nation has reported any erosion of the atmosphere of free speech or debate. At the same time, the United States, which until recently has refused to put such rules into effect, has a less than perfect record of protecting even political speech. We persecuted communists, hounded Hollywood writers out of the country, and harassed and badgered such civil rights leaders as Josephine Baker, Paul Robeson, and W.E.B. DuBois in a campaign of personal and professional smears that ruined their reputations and denied them the ability to make a living. In recent times, conservatives inside and outside the Administration have disparaged progressives to the point where many are now afraid to use the "liberal" word to describe themselves. Controversial artists are denied federal funding. Museum exhibits that depict the A-bombing of Hiroshima have been ordered modified. If political speech lies at the center of the First Amendment, its protection seems to be largely independent of what is taking place at the periphery. There may, indeed, be an inverse correlation. Those institutions most concerned with social fairness have proved to be the ones most likely to promulgate anti-hate-speech rules. Part of the reason seems to be recognition that hate speech can easily silence and demoralize its victims, discouraging them from participating in the life of the institution. If so, enacting hate-speech rules may be evidence of a commitment to democratic dialogue, rather than the opposite, as some of their opponents maintain.

Richard Delgado and Jean Stefancic, *Must We Defend Nazis?* 1997.

There may be free speech for racists advocating police "racial profiling," but not free speech for victims of racism, police harassment and brutality. The victims are slandered and convicted either by the police being judge, jury and executioner or by the mass media in their court of racist coverage. Free speech has a class line. It also has a class responsibility. One person's beliefs cannot cross the line into threats of violence. Free speech does not cover that. Those kinds of terrorist acts threaten everyone's free speech. It creates a chilling effect on public discussion when the hate mongers call for killing based on race, national origin, religion, who one loves or whether you provide or seek a legal medical procedure. It is only in the ruling class and corporate interests that these terrorist groups are allowed to exist.

Not a Violation of Free Speech

That's why not allowing the Klan to march or jailing White Aryan Resistance leader, Tom Metzger, for his public calls for violence is not a violation of freedom of speech. Those acts will, in fact, deepen and broaden freedom of speech by "de-terrorizing" the atmosphere.

The Communist Party constantly gets letters, calls and e-mail from thousands across the country who are intimidated by these forces and can't speak their views and organize according to their beliefs because of the terrorist ultra-right groups, be it militia or neo-Nazi, because of the atmosphere they create. This atmosphere of fear is a direct assault on freedom of speech.

The majority of American people are seeing this class divide. It is evident in the majority opinion in favor of hate crimes legislation. It is evident by the majority opinion against violence and hate speech based on race, nationality, status, sexual orientation or religion.

Outlaw Hate Groups

It is in the interests of the overwhelming majority in our country to outlaw groups of racism, hate and terror. In the name of human decency and democracy their existence cannot be allowed to continue. The government knows who these groups are but it's up to a united coalition of white,

Black, Latino, Asian, American Indian, Pacific Islander, Middle Eastern, men and women, gay and straight, Jewish, Christian, Muslim, Buddhist, Hindu and atheist, immigrant and U.S. born, and people's organizations—trade unions, civil rights, religious, peace, women's and elected officials to struggle and force the government to act.

Does outlawing racist, anti-Semitic, bigoted hate groups make racism or bigotry go away? No. But it is a giant step in democratizing public discourse and free speech. And it is a giant step in making all our lives and the lives of our children safer.

> *"More and more people really believe that they have a right not to be offended or have their feelings hurt, and that that supposed right is more important than the right to free speech."*

Hate Speech Should Not Be Banned

William L. Pierce

William L. Pierce is the founder of the National Alliance, a white supremacist group. He also wrote, under the pseudonym Andrew Macdonald, *The Turner Diaries*. The following viewpoint was excerpted from his weekly radio program and reprinted in his monthly online magazine *Free Speech*. Turner argues that a movement is growing in the United States that would ban any word or action that may offend someone. As hurtful as hate speech may be to its victims, Turner contends, the U.S. Constitution guarantees people the right to be offensive. Americans must be willing to fight to preserve their right to freedom of speech, he asserts.

As you read, consider the following questions:

1. What do politically correct people mean when they say that the First Amendment was not meant to protect offensive speech, according to Pierce?
2. What is the agenda of the "feel-good" faction, in the author's opinion?
3. According to the author, what will spur the politicians into restricting free speech?

Reprinted from "Hate Speech," by William L. Pierce, *Free Speech*, November 1995, by permission of *Free Speech*.

I've spoken often with you about the Jewish monopoly control of our mass media of news and entertainment. Recently I detailed the takeover of the Disney company by Jews and its conversion into an instrument of brainwashing used against young Americans.

A Subversive Campaign

In addition to this consolidation of Jewish control over the media, there's another subversive campaign underway in this country which is just as dangerous for our future. It's the campaign to stifle any expression of opinion except those coming from the Jew-controlled mass media: the campaign to outlaw all dissident voices.

When I've mentioned this campaign in the past, some people have thought I was being an alarmist. They believe that freedom of speech is too deeply rooted in American soil to be done away with by a few extremists in the Clinton administration, or any administration. The American people won't tolerate having their freedom of speech taken away, they believe.

I wish that I could share their optimism. What makes it difficult for me to do so is the fact that there is a growing body of opinion in America that no one should have the right to do or say anything which offends someone else. The people who believe this are not only entrenched in the Clinton administration, they're entrenched in the Congress, in the universities, and in many other American institutions. These people will tell you with a straight face that the First Amendment was never meant to protect offensive speech— or what they more often these days call—*hate speech*. The Constitution doesn't give anyone the right to hurt someone else's feelings, they say. It doesn't give anyone the right to offend someone else. It doesn't give anyone the right to say unkind things about someone else, so that other people might be influenced by what is said and then in turn think or say unkind things themselves—perhaps even do something unkind.

Actually, what these Politically Correct people really mean, although they won't tell you this—what they really mean is that no one should be permitted to write or say anything which might offend one of the officially favored classes of people: homosexuals, morally or physically defective people, Jews, Blacks or members of other non-White racial groups, and women. They see nothing wrong with offending a White male, for example: they do it themselves all the time. But they do believe that it ought to be illegal to do or say something offensive to almost anyone else. . . .

Offensive Words

Perhaps I should say at this point that I understand what it means to be offended and to have one's feelings hurt. I've worn glasses since I was five years old, and it used to hurt my feelings when some of my school classmates would call me "four eyes." I used to do pretty well in my school work too, and as a result occasionally one of the kids who didn't do so well would refer to me sneeringly as "Einstein." That really made me feel uncomfortable.

And I'm sure it's uncomfortable for a person who's overweight to hear herself called "fatso." I'm sure it makes a retarded person feel bad to be told he's stupid. I'm sure that a person who's not attractive doesn't like to be reminded of that fact.

But, you know, that's life. We all put up with a lot of things we don't like. We try to make the best of it. If we're fat and we don't like being called fatso, we try to lose some weight. If we're nearsighted and have to wear glasses, perhaps we can switch to contact lenses—or take karate lessons and punch out anybody who calls us "four eyes."

There's really something seriously wrong with the people who believe that it should be illegal to hurt a homosexual's feelings, or to stare at a pretty girl—or to call a person who wears glasses "four eyes," for that matter. Some of these people clearly believe that it's more important for us all to be able to feel good about ourselves all the time than it is for us to be free.

Pushing an Agenda

And some of these people are simply using the "feel-good" faction to push their own agenda, which is to make it impossible for the few people who have figured out what they're up to tell the rest of the people. They want to make it illegal to tell people about the Jewish control of the news and entertainment media, for example. They want to make it illegal for this program to be on the air. They call this program "hate radio," because it is offensive to them.

Laws Do Not Stop Hate

The Supreme Court has been wary of a general proscription of hate speech. . . .

Even if laws that the Supreme Court would abide could be crafted, however, there is another, more difficult, problem for the advocates of such laws: they don't stop hate. That is the fundamental flaw in solutions that focus on hate speech laws. The proponents of such laws frequently fail to disentangle three distinct issues: hate speech, hate crimes, and the silencing of victim groups. Hate causes each of these. It does not necessarily follow that hate speech causes either hate crimes or the silencing of victim groups or that anti-hate speech laws will relieve either problem. Censoring hate speech may have emotional and symbolic appeal but little if any utility as a solution.

Paul McMasters, *Human Rights*, Fall 1999.

What makes me worry so much is that the "feel-good" faction is growing. There's something unhealthy about life in America today, and it's making more and more people really believe that they have a right not to be offended or have their feelings hurt, and that that supposed right is more important than the right to free speech. And the folks who are taking advantage of this sickness by pushing the idea that offensive speech or hate speech ought to be outlawed are becoming more pushy in their efforts.

The Turner Diaries

Back in 1978 I wrote a novel which I called *The Turner Diaries*. It's a novel about life in the United States as I imagined it might be in the 1990s, if some of the trends I could see in the 1970s continued for another 20 years. I imagined that the government would become more repressive, and it has. I imagined that most of the people would react in a sheeplike way to government repression and would not complain as long as they could still be comfortable and feel good, and that's the way it's turned out. And I imagined that a few people would not react like sheep, but instead would fight back violently—and a few have. In writing my novel, I really tried to be realistic, and to speak my mind completely. I didn't rewrite any part of my book or leave out any part because I thought it might be offensive to some people—and, of course, it has been.

I have a clipping here from the *Jewish Press*, which is published in New York City and which describes itself as the world's largest circulation English-language Jewish newspaper. It's a story about what the folks at the *Jewish Press* see as a need to "close the loopholes in the U.S. Constitution," as they so nicely put it. And it's a story about the novel I wrote. I'll read you a couple of paragraphs from this story in the *Jewish Press*:

> The radical right is taking advantage of the Republican victory in Congress to push its own agenda in defiance of the principles that have made the United States a haven for persecuted minorities, a beacon of freedom, justice, and liberty to all people. Unfortunately, the man-made laws under which we operate are like a two-edged sword, offering opportunity to all elements of society to achieve their goals but also similar rights for all to speak their minds even when it contravenes the very essence of tolerance and democracy. One glaring example of this attempt to exploit the loopholes in the U.S. Constitution to bring prejudice and racism in their most vicious forms to public attention is the publication in 1978 of a book called *The Turner Diaries* by Andrew Macdonald, the pseudonym of William L. Pierce, a former professor of physics and research scientist . . . . Pierce's book, which surpasses *Mein Kampf* in its virulent anti-Semitism, has sold more than 187,000 copies. It describes an end-of-the-century scenario in which the Jewish dominated government is overthrown by the Organization, an underground white group which succeeds where Nazism failed. . . . Our first reaction . . . is that even in the United States there must be a limit to such abuse of so-called freedom of speech. We have enough experience with vicious racists to justify some control over their actions.

Did you note the phrase "so-called freedom of speech"? These folks at the *Jewish Press* really would like for the government to prohibit the writing and publication of novels with plots they find offensive or hateful.

Cause and Effect

I have another newspaper clipping, this one from the *Fulton County Daily Report*. It's an editorial written by two radical feminists, one a law professor and the other a law student at Northwestern University. Like the *Jewish Press* these two women also focus on my novel *The Turner Diaries*. They urge that the laws of our land be changed so that I and others who write books they find offensive can be prosecuted—or at least sued for the damage they claim our writing causes. In my case, they allege that the person or persons who blew up the federal building in Oklahoma City in 1995 were caused to do so by reading *The Turner Diaries*, and so therefore I should be sued for all of the deaths and property loss caused by that act. And, of course, the same for other books which they allege caused people to do harmful things or which offend people—and, believe me, these women and their friends on the Human Rights Councils are *easily* offended. And they are quick to see a cause-and-effect relationship between written words or an image in a book and criminal acts by people who read those words. They take it for granted that literature which they consider demeaning to women causes men to rape women. I'll read you just a little of their article:

> Even under current constitutional law, all speech is not equally protected regardless of content. The test is whether the harm caused by the speech is so grave that it outweighs the benefits of protecting its authors from liability. Usually the answer is no. This delicate balancing of interests, however, depends upon judgments about the severity of the harm, not on some absolute legal protection for all things written. Wrapping William Pierce in the fabric of the First Amendment ensures that there is a class of harms occasioned by violent and hate-filled images—insults, threats, beatings, rapes, and killings—that remain immune from ordinary legal consequence, even when cause and effect are plainly evident. In reality, if not in First Amendment theory, there persists a connection between image, incitement, and violence: cross-burnings and lynchings, yellow stars and deportations, pornography and rape, *The Turner Diaries* and Oklahoma City.

Well, it's pretty clear what these two feminists have in mind, even if they don't come right out and say it. They want to make it illegal for you or for me to insult or offend them or someone in solidarity with them—or, barring that, they want to be able to sue us for saying something which hurts the feelings of an AIDS carrier or a homosexual or a feminist or a member of one of the other officially protected minorities. They say, in effect, "Look, if we let William Pierce get away with writing books like *The Turner Diaries* just because of this obsolete legal fiction called the First Amendment, then we'll also have to put up with all sorts of other insults and hate-filled images."

I don't know what sort of insults have so rankled these two feminist lawyers, but it's pretty clear that they're rankled. I wouldn't worry about that so much, except that I'm afraid that the number of feel-good trendies who'll fall for their argument to abolish the First Amendment is growing. Worse than that, I worry that too many of the rest of us will just sit on our hands and let the anti-Constitutional lynch mob have its way.

Free Speech and Politicians

And, you know, politicians keep up with these trends too. They read the newspapers. They take polls. If they believe that the majority of Americans will fight to keep their rights, then the politicians won't mess with them. They'll even make speeches about how much they love the Constitution, and especially the First Amendment. But as soon as they figure that the people won't fight for their rights, they'll be leading the lynch mob and making speeches about the need to protect people from being offended or harmed by hateful speech.

And what I've just said applies to nearly all politicians and their camp followers. . . . It applies to Republicans and conservatives at least as much as it applies to Democrats and liberals. I have another newspaper article, with an essay by Robert Bork, the very conservative legal scholar who was hounded out of his Supreme Court nomination a few years ago because of his conservatism. Mr. Bork now says that we need to reinterpret the First Amendment, so that it does not protect hateful speech. I don't know what appointment Mr. Bork has his eye on now, but that's what the man is saying.

It all boils down to this: Nobody in this country, or anywhere else, has any *inalienable* rights: not the right to free speech or freedom of religion or assembly, not the right to keep and bear arms, not the right to be free from unreasonable searches and seizures. There always will be scoundrels who will try to take away your rights if they believe they can get away with it. And there always will be fools who will let them do it. The only rights that we have, the only rights that we can depend on, are those that we are willing and able to fight for, to shed blood for. And that's what it's coming to in this country very soon.

Now you've heard it. Now I want you think about it. And then I want you to start getting ready for what's coming.

> *"Respect for God and country are basic to what our nation stands for and are ideals worth honoring and protecting."*

Flag Desecration Should Be Banned

Tommy Lasorda

Tommy Lasorda is the general manager of the Los Angeles Dodgers. In the following viewpoint, which is taken from his testimony before a congressional committee in 1998, Lasorda argues that the American flag is an important symbol of America, and as such, it should be protected from acts of desecration such as burning. He urges Congress to pass an amendment that prohibits flag burning and other acts of physical desecration. As of May 2001, the amendment had not passed both houses in Congress.

As you read, consider the following questions:
1. What is one of the greatest ideas that Americans can teach their children, in Lasorda's opinion?
2. According to Lasorda, who took away the people's right to protect their flag?
3. How many acts of flag desecration were reported during an eighteen-month period, as cited by the author?

Reprinted from Tommy Lasorda's testimony before the U.S. Senate Committee on the Judiciary, July 8, 1998.

Mr. Chairman and members of the committee. Thank you for allowing me to speak today in support of . . . an amendment to protect our flag from acts of physical desecration.

My name is Tommy Lasorda and I am the general manager of the Los Angeles Dodgers. Nearly five decades ago, I began living a dream as I embarked on a career that allowed me to be a part of the great American pastime as a major league player, coach, and manager for the world-famous Los Angeles Dodgers.

Historic Moments in Baseball

Not only have I lived every school boy's dream, but I have also been present during a number of historic moments that have brought the country together in a way that few other events can.

During the 1977 World Series, Reggie Jackson hit four towering home runs on four consecutive pitches to lead the enemy Yankees past my Dodgers for the World Championship.

On September 28, 1988, Dodger great Orel Hershiser needed 10 scoreless innings to top the record for consecutive scoreless innings set in 1968 by Don Drysdale. Locked in a scoreless pitcher's duel with the San Diego Padres, sports fans from around the country tuned in to watch Hershiser break this long-standing record.

In the first game of the 1988 World Series against the Oakland Athletics, I called upon injured Dodger Kirk Gibson to pinch-hit in the bottom of the ninth inning against the unhittable Dennis Eckersley. As many Americans remember, Gibson, in his only at-bat of the series, hit a home run to cap a dramatic come-from-behind win and propel us to a World Championship.

As I look back at the American history I have been privileged enough to be a part of, I can't help thinking about the other part of our American pastime that holds us all together—the respect we show for each other, and the nation, when we take off our caps, face the American flag, and sing the national anthem before every major league game. For you see, baseball, like the American flag and national anthem, ties everyone in this great country of ours together.

I am here today for a number of reasons. First, because I proudly served this great country in the Army's Special Service unit from 1946 to 1947. And because when I travel the country for the Dodgers and watch the news, I am reminded that one of the greatest things we can teach the children of tomorrow—respect for God and country—is getting more and more difficult to pass on.

One of the best ways we can teach this respect is by protecting our flag from physical desecration. Too many Americans do not realize that the Supreme Court in 1989, by just one vote, declared that this behavior is protected "speech" under the First Amendment. Five judges took away the right of the people to protect their flag—a right exercised since our birth, defended by the Justices on five previous Supreme Courts, and by James Madison and Thomas Jefferson who helped adopt the first flag and write the First Amendment.

Flag Desecrations

Today, because of the Supreme Court's decision, the flag is just another piece of cloth that can be burned and soiled with impunity.

In the rotunda of the state capital in Lansing, Michigan, a young man wiped his rear end with the American flag at the Governor's State of the State Address. The event was taped by the NBC affiliate as the crowd chanted, "What do we want? Revolution. When do we want it? Now." Police stood by and watched because the courts say this behavior is "free speech."

In Wallingford, Connecticut, a young man burned American flags and poured red paint over a church's statue of the Virgin Mary, breaking off the thumb and cracking the upper portion of the monument.

In Lafayette Square [in Washington, D.C.], just a few blocks from where we sit today, 2,000 angry protestors raised their voices against the Clinton administration's stand against Iraqi president Saddam Hussein by carrying anti-war banners and burning the American flag.

In a small Wisconsin town, a high school student pulled down the American flag from a golf course, defecated on it, and left it on the steps of the club house. The district attorney tried to prosecute the young man, but the judge threw it out because defecating on the flag is "free speech."

Contrast these occurrences with one of the most heroic acts ever to take place on the field during a Major League Baseball game.

Public Opinion Supports an Amendment Against Flag Desecration

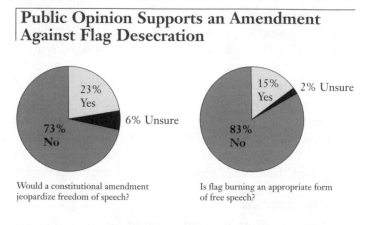

Would a constitutional amendment jeopardize freedom of speech?

Is flag burning an appropriate form of free speech?

Consistent tracking of public opinion confirms the broad-based, overwhelming support American voters have for an amendment to the U.S. Constitution to protect the American flag from desecration. After interviewing nearly 8,500 American voters, roughly three-quarters of voters across all demographic and geographic subgroups would personally vote for a Flag Protection Amendment.

Citizens Flag Alliance, public opinion poll, May 1997.

On April 25, 1976, as we played the Chicago Cubs at Dodger Stadium, I witnessed a flag burning. In the middle of the fourth inning, as the fielders were warming up, two protestors ran onto the field. The men quickly ran past left fielder Jose Cardenal and stopped in left-center field. One of the men stooped to his knees, unscrewed the cap to a can of lighter fluid, and soaked the American flag with it. We all watched dumbstruck as the man pulled out a match and tried to light the American flag on fire.

To the astonishment of the protestors, the fans, and those of us on the field, all-star outfielder Rick Monday ran at the protestors, grabbed the burning flag and ran towards the dugout, as I screamed at the protestors from the third-base coaching box.

The fans immediately got on their feet to recognize Monday's heroic act. And without any prompting that I can remember, the whole crowd stood and began to fill the stadium with an impromptu rendition of "God Bless America."

Burning the Flag Is Wrong

News outlets around the country included the highlight that night on the evening news. Twenty years later, *The Sporting News* commemorated the event. Today, the flag burning incident is still shown in highlights. And everyone who saw the incident then, and now, knows that the protestors were doing something terrible, offensive, and wrong.

People on the other side of this issue will try to tell you that flag desecration or events like the ones I just described don't happen often enough, aren't offensive enough, or that they just aren't a big deal. They don't believe that 20 acts of flag desecration in the last 18 months is very many. But these people are wrong, just like the protestors that day in Dodger Stadium were.

It is not how often a flag is desecrated that makes it wrong. Just because cross burnings don't happen every day, doesn't mean that they are no longer wrong. If your son or daughter is caught breaking the law, do you tell them that what they did was not wrong because they'd never done it before?

In poll after poll, more than 80 percent of Americans say that they want this amendment; several statewide polls show similar results. In addition, legislatures in 49 states have passed resolutions urging Congress to pass the flag protection amendment.

By joining the House in passing the amendment, the Senate can protect an honored symbol that ties every American together, while preserving our First Amendment rights. You can also send a very important message to the young people of this country—that respect for God and country are basic to what our nation stands for and are ideals worth honoring and protecting.

I urge you to help teach our children about these ideals by passing this amendment and sending it to the states for ratification.

"A nation that uses force to compel unity and patriotism is a nation on its way to a dictatorship."

Flag Desecration Should Not Be Banned

Charles Levendosky

Charles Levendosky is the editor of the *Casper (Wyoming) Star-Tribune* editorial page and a noted columnist on First Amendment issues. In the following viewpoint, Levendosky argues that burning the American flag is a form of political speech, and as such, is protected under the First Amendment. Prohibiting flag burning, he contends, risks turning the flag into a symbol more sacred than any religious icon and the United States into a dictatorship.

As you read, consider the following questions:
1. What was the Supreme Court's ruling in *Texas v. Johnson*, as cited by the author?
2. What was Ivan Warner's response to an assertion by a North Vietnamese officer that his cause was wrong because some Americans were protesting the war?
3. How would a flag be treated compared to some religious symbol if a flag amendment was passed, in Levendosky's opinion?

Reprinted, with permission, from "There's Great Danger in Raising the Flag So High," by Charles Levendosky, *Liberal Opinion Weekly*, April 26, 1999.

The "Flag Uber Alles" [over all] boys are at it again. They want to raise the American flag above the U.S. Constitution and the Bill of Rights. In doing so they raise it to the level of idolatry.

Members of both houses of Congress have introduced amendments to the Constitution "authorizing Congress to prohibit the physical desecration of the flag of the United States.". . .

Those who support the flag desecration amendment say it doesn't violate the First Amendment's protection of political dissent. Flag burning, they contend, isn't speech.

Political Protest

Funny isn't it, these same folks got the message back in 1984 when Gregory Lee Johnson doused an American flag with kerosene and set it on fire? He did so in front of city hall in Dallas during the Republican National Convention. Texas charged Johnson with desecration of a venerated object and sentenced him to one year in prison. He won at the Texas Court of Criminal Appeals and later (1989) at the U.S. Supreme Court, by a narrow majority.

Funny isn't it, that flag etiquette provides for burning a tattered or soiled flag. So how do these flag amendment folks distinguish a desecration from veneration? By context, of course. And the message is extremely, if offensively, clear when flag burning is political protest.

The Supreme Court is nearly unanimous in accepting that flag burning in certain contexts expresses a message of dissent. Justice William Brennan who wrote for the majority in *Texas vs. Johnson*, stated, "If there is a bedrock of principle underlying the First Amendment, it is that the government may not prohibit the expression of an idea simply because society finds the idea itself offensive or disagreeable."

Brennan ended the opinion: "Our decision is a reaffirmation of the principles of freedom and inclusiveness that the flag best reflects, and of the conviction that our tolerance of criticism such as Johnson's is a sign and source of our strength. . . . The way to preserve the flag's special role is not to punish those who feel differently about these matters. It is to persuade them that they are wrong." He ends this paragraph: "We do not consecrate the flag by punishing its desecration, for in doing so we dilute the freedom that this cherished emblem represents."

Free to Protest

Ivan Warner, a veteran of the Vietnam War who received the Silver Star and two Purple Hearts, was imprisoned by the North Vietnamese from 1967 to 1973. He is quoted by Nat Hentoff in his book *Free Speech for Me—But Not for Thee* telling about his captives. His words give specificity to Brennan's more general truth, "our tolerance of criticism . . . is a sign and source of our strength."

Warner said, "I remember one interrogation where I was shown a photograph of some Americans protesting the war by burning the flag. 'There,' the officer said. 'People in your country protest against your cause. That proves you are wrong.'"

FIGHTING FIRE WITH FIRE

Warner countered, "No. That proves that I am right. In my country, we are not afraid of freedom, even if it means that people disagree with us." Warner went on to say, "The officer was on his feet in an instant, his face purple with rage.

He smashed his fist onto the table and screamed at me to shut up. While he was ranting, I was astonished to see pain, compounded by fear, in his eyes. I have never forgotten that look, nor have I forgotten the satisfaction I felt at using his tool, the picture of the burning flag, against him."

A nation that uses force to compel unity and patriotism is a nation on its way to a dictatorship.

These Flag Uber Alles advocates raise the flag above the very liberties it represents. No nation has protected political dissent more than the United States—yet this amendment would strangle some forms of political protest. We are a nation born of a revolution, our founders understood all forms of political protest must be protected. That was the intent of the First Amendment's all encompassing protection: "Congress shall make no law abridging . . . the freedom of speech."

A Graven Image?

If the flag is raised so high that it is sacred compared to the Constitution and the Bill of Rights, there is the danger that it becomes a graven image, akin to a religious idol.

It isn't against the law to burn a cross or any other religious symbol—yet it would be against the law to burn a flag, if these flag amendment folks have their way. The implication here is that the flag is more important (More sacred?) than any religious symbol. Many will find that notion offensive.

Congress should drop this phony pretence at patriotism and get down to the important work that the people sent them to Washington, D.C. to accomplish—solving the problems of Social Security and universal medical care. Grappling and dealing with those real problems should be patriotism enough for any politician.

*"Saying that abortion is wrong and should
be outlawed is political speech. Suggesting
that doctors who provide abortions should
be killed is not."*

The Free Speech Rights of Abortion Protesters Should Be Restricted

Richard Curtis

The Nuremberg Files was a website established by anti-abortion activists that publicized the names, addresses, and other personal information of abortion providers. In the following viewpoint, Richard Curtis argues that the abortion protesters violated the First Amendment because their website went beyond political speech against abortion and effectively made threats against people, which are not protected speech. Curtis is a frequent contributor to *People's Weekly World*, a publication of the Communist Party U.S.A.

As you read, consider the following questions:
1. How did Planned Parenthood perceive the "Wanted" posters found on the Nuremberg Files' website, according to the Associated Press?
2. Where should the line be drawn between being disagreeable and being a terrorist, according to Curtis?
3. What is the cornerstone of American democracy, in the author's opinion?

Reprinted, with permission, from "Is It Terrorism or Just Free Speech Like They Claim?" by Richard Curtis, *People's Weekly World*, February 13, 1999.

"Wanted" posters and a Web site listing names and addresses of "baby butchers" amount to illegal threats, and the anti-abortion activists who created them must pay $107 million in damages, a federal jury says.

"The jury saw the posters for what they are—a hit list for terrorists," said Gloria Feldt, president of Planned Parenthood, which joined several abortion doctors and a clinic in suing the activists.

—Associated Press 2/3/99

In the legal case the issue was whether a "reasonable" person would find the material threatening. This was the standard of proof required by the judge in this case.

The Supreme Court has in the past used another, more liberal standard (from the perspective of the terrorists anyway) that the speech in question must be likely to cause "imminent lawless action."

In philosophy there is an old saying that goes something like this: If a thing walks like a duck, looks like a duck, and sounds like a duck then it is a duck. Which is to say that if a reasonable person would take a thing to be a duck, one might safely conclude that it is a duck.

Threatening Speech

If fanatical terrorists are threatening medical professionals with the claim that these medical professionals ought to be eliminated, then these fanatical terrorists are not merely engaging in constitutionally protected free speech.

If it sounds like a threat and is taken by an outside observer to be a threat, and thus acts like a threat, then it is a threat.

Some alleged First Amendment scholars have claimed that the ruling goes too far. The claim is that the principle of the Constitution is that which we as a society must tolerate all political speech, including that we might find offensive.

In short, one has a constitutionally protected right to believe and say things that any sane person would find absurd or disturbing. But where is the line between being disagreeable and being a terrorist?

One has to wonder about the people who find this a difficult question. If the purpose of one's speech is a dialogue about political questions, then it is protected free speech; if one's purpose is to force changes in other people's behavior through an implicit or overt threat of violence, then one is a terrorist.

Death Threats Are Not Protected Speech

Terrorizing doctors is not a free speech issue and maintaining a database with personal information and encouraging others to use that information for nefarious purposes—i.e. murder—is clearly threatening.

Look at it this way. These terrorists also disagree with politicians who support the right of women to control their own fertility—politicians like Bill Clinton.

And if the terrorist enterprise in question maintained a database that included a call to eliminate the president and had information about his movements that would allow a particularly dedicated terrorist to act on that threat what would happen?

Not Protected Speech

Robyn Blumner wrote in the February 10, 1999, *Wall Street Journal* that the words on the antiabortion Web site in Oregon were "no worse than neo-Nazi calls for the annihilation of the Jewish people." But Ira Glasser, executive director of the American Civil Liberties Union, in a February 17, 1999, letter to the *Wall Street Journal* answers: "It is one thing to say that all abortion providers deserve to die. It is quite another to publish detailed information on wanted posters about particular doctors—their photos, names, cars (with license plates), home addresses, names of children, where their children go to school, etc.—and then triumphantly cross out their names when particular doctors are killed."

I am pro-life. . . . I am also a supporter of free speech across the board. . . .

Caught between these two allegiances in the Oregon Web site case, I agree with the jury's verdict that the posters and the Web site are *not* protected speech.

Nat Hentoff, *Village Voice*, June 1, 1999.

The Secret Service would, quite reasonably, shut the web site down and arrest everyone involved for threatening a government official.

There is no constitutionally protected right to threaten the president. So where is the gray area in this case? Saying that abortion is wrong and should be outlawed is political speech. Suggesting that doctors who provide abortions should be killed is not.

It cannot be clearer than that, but right-wing politicians and the people who support them are very clever and slippery. They will try to make a case that putting out "wanted," posters is not a threat.

These same people, and even some liberals who might be well intentioned, will also argue that sending people unsolicited swastikas in the mail is free speech. The right wing works with terror and fear. Without fear there would never be support for right-wing politics.

And so they will always argue for an absurd standard of proof that allows their violent side to threaten people.

The other side of all this is that we, as Americans, also have a right to live without threats. The freedom of speech carries with it a duty to use that right for legitimate purposes.

A Threat to Democracy

Those who intentionally misuse this right to free speech are a threat to the democratic character of the nation and we all thus have a corresponding duty to stop them.

Freedom of speech is the cornerstone of our democracy, which is why it is first in the Bill of Rights. Those who abuse this right are a threat not just to those being terrorized but are a threat to the very fabric of democracy. It is good and just that these anti-choice fanatics are stopped.

Hopefully, this case will eventually put a stop to their organized activity and some day provide the legal framework for stopping the maniacs who use the cover of the First Amendment to distribute racist propaganda as a way of threatening people.

"[Speech] should be protected regardless of whether abortion doctors felt at physical risk, as long as its authors never intended to incite violence."

The Free Speech Rights of Abortion Protesters Should Not Be Restricted

Robyn Blumner

The abortion protesters who were behind the Nuremberg Files—a website that publicized personal information about abortion providers—were engaging in protected speech and should not have been found guilty of making threats, argues Robyn Blumner in the following viewpoint. The protesters did not make any explicit threats of violence against the abortion providers, she contends, and therefore their speech is protected. A verdict that finds that the protesters should have known that the doctors would feel threatened by the website places an unmanageable burden upon the speaker to know what an audience is thinking. Blumner is a syndicated columnist and editorial writer for the *St. Petersburg Times*.

As you read, consider the following questions:
1. How is the case *NAACP v. Clairborne Hardware* similar to that of the Nuremberg Files in Portland, Oregon, according to Blumner?
2. How is the NAACP case different from the Nuremberg Files?
3. On what does the future of freedom of speech depend, in Blumner's view?

A nti-abortion protesters who employ tactics similar to those used by the civil rights movement are getting a very different reception in court.

The Case

Nothing could illustrate this more starkly than the out-of-sight $107-million in damages awarded in February 1999 to Planned Parenthood and a group of doctors who perform abortions. Fourteen anti-abortion activists were found to have violated the federal Freedom of Access to Clinic Entrances Act by threatening abortion providers with physical harm, even though there were no explicit threats of violence at issue.

The federal jury in Portland, Oregon, found that the protesters broke the law by putting up "Wanted" posters charging abortion doctors with "crimes against humanity," and by creating a Web site titled "The Nuremberg Files" that lists names, addresses and other personal information about abortion doctors and strikes through their names with a black line if they have been killed. The reason for the jury verdict was not that the doctors had been harmed or even that the obnoxious Web site in itself threatened violence. The reason was that the material made the doctors feel threatened in the context of the ongoing violence against abortion providers, and, under the law, all the jury had to discern was whether it was reasonable for the authors to have known they would.

Yet, if First Amendment precedent had been followed, this case would never have even gotten in front of a jury, says UCLA law professor Eugene Volokh, who specializes in free speech law. That's because it closely resembles a case in which the U.S. Supreme Court granted constitutional protection to speech that created a menacing atmosphere in the context of a broad public debate.

A Similar Case

In the case of *NAACP vs. Clairborne Hardware*, local leaders in Clairborne County, Mississippi, refused to respond to the demands of black residents. Those demands included desegregating public schools, hiring black police officers and adding blacks to juries. In response, the NAACP organized a boycott of white-owned businesses, which lasted from 1966 to 1973.

To pressure fellow black citizens to respect the boycott, Charles Evers, the NAACP field secretary in Mississippi, made a number of fiery speeches, in which he warned that blacks would be answerable to him if they patronized white businesses. According to one account, he told his audience, "Uncle Toms" who broke the boycott would "have their necks broken by their own people."

Reprinted by permission of Chuck Asay and Creators Syndicate.

In addition to the threatening speeches, a group of "enforcers" or "black hats" was organized to stand guard at white-owned businesses and record the names of blacks frequenting them. Those names were then published in the *Black Times* and read aloud at NAACP meetings. Although for most boycott violators the extent of their punishment was being called demeaning names, for as many as 10 people reprisals took a more violent form. In one case, a man was beaten, and, in another case, a man was whipped with his pants pulled down.

The businesses sued over the boycott, claiming, among

other things, that the use of violence, intimidation and an atmosphere of fear constituted tortious interference in their businesses. Though they won a large damage award in Mississippi courts, the case was overturned by the U.S. Supreme Court. In absolving the NAACP, Evers and all other defendants of liability, the high court declared that the "emotionally charged rhetoric of Charles Evers' speeches did not transcend the bounds of protected speech," nor did the practices of the "black hats" in publicly naming boycott violators.

The court concluded that the only people who should be liable for damages were those who specifically participated in the violent activities or incited imminent lawless action. And it reiterated that "mere advocacy of the use of force or violence does not remove speech from the protection of the First Amendment."

"To rule otherwise," said the court, "would ignore the 'profound national commitment' that 'debate on public issues should be uninhibited, robust, and wide open.'"

Compare that result to the one obtained in the Oregon courtroom—where the inflamed and impassioned rhetoric of anti-abortion activists speaking on a divisive public issue was found to have no sanctuary in the First Amendment. Naming names of abortion doctors was deemed an implied threat of violence, but naming civil rights boycott violators was free speech. The explicit threats of violence made by NAACP officials were placed in the appropriately broader context of speech; the Web site of anti-abortion activists was deemed assaultive.

The Case's Effects

So what does this mean for the future of activism? Does it mean that Greenpeace can't post a list of polluting companies' CEOs? Does it mean that Nazi hunters can be barred from publishing the names of former Nazis who are living in this country? Does it mean convicted sex offenders can collect millions of dollars from anyone who alerts the neighborhoods where they now live? Since, in each instance those named may feel physically threatened, and the publishers of their names could foresee that.

The future of freedom of speech depends upon courts

caring less about how a listener receives a message than what a speaker meant to convey. The Web site and posters should be protected regardless of whether abortion doctors felt at physical risk, as long as its authors never intended to incite violence. But the Oregon ruling lets the listeners' reactions to speech control what gets said. It is now up to the speaker to temper his remarks to avoid being misconstrued—or face bankruptcy.

Good thing this wasn't the standard during the civil rights movement, or there might never have been one.

Periodical Bibliography

The following articles have been selected to supplement the diverse views presented in this chapter. Addresses are provided for periodicals not indexed in the *Readers' Guide to Periodical Literature*, the *Alternative Press Index*, the *Social Sciences Index*, or the *Index to Legal Periodicals and Books*.

Robyn Blumner	"ACLU Backs Free Speech for All—Except Pro-Lifers," *The New York Times*, February 10, 1999.
Adam Cohen	"Cyberspeech on Trial," *Time*, February 15, 1999.
Michael Cromartie	"Give Me Liberty, but Don't Give Me Filth," *Christianity Today*, May 19, 1997.
Alan M. Dershowitz	"Baseball's Speech Police," *The New York Times*, February 2, 2000.
Edward McGlynn Gaffney Jr.	"Protesting Abortion," *Commonweal*, March 26, 1999.
William Gass	"Shears of the Censor," *Harper's*, April 1997.
John Leo	"Dissing John Rocker," *U.S. News & World Report*, February 14, 2000.
Neil A. Lewis	"Switching Sides on Free Speech," *The New York Times*, April 26, 1998.
David Lowenthal	"The Case for Censorship," *Weekly Standard*, August 23, 1999. Available from 1150 17th St. NW, Suite 505, Washington, DC 20036-4617.
Sam Howe Verhovek	"Creators of Anti-Abortion Web Site Told to Pay Millions," *The New York Times*, February 3, 1999.
Eugene Volokh	"Taxation Isn't Censorship," *Wall Street Journal*, March 23, 2000.
Jonathan D. Wallace	"Pervasive Problem," *Reason*, October 1998.
Geoffrey Wheatcroft	"Lock Up the Holocaust Deniers?" *The New York Times*, October 12, 1998.
Armstrong Williams	"Conduct Unbecoming Free Speech," *American Legion*, July 1998. Available from PO Box 1055, Indianapolis, IN 46206.
Wilson Quarterly	"One Cheer for Censorship," Winter 2000.

CHAPTER 2

Should Pornography Be Censored?

Chapter Preface

The growth of the World Wide Web has provided enormous educational opportunities for students. However, it has also led to the proliferation of cyberporn that can be easily found by anyone—including children—who has Internet access. In recent years, Congress has attempted to protect children from being inadvertently exposed to pornography online.

One of the first efforts to regulate online pornography was the Communications Decency Act (CDA) of 1995. The act prohibited the display or transmission of obscene or indecent material over the Internet to minors, but exempted from prosecution those who had made a good-faith effort to prevent minors from viewing the objectionable material. However, the Supreme Court struck down the CDA in 1997, ruling that the terms of the law would "cover large amounts of non-pornographic material with serious educational or other value," and that therefore the act placed "an unacceptably heavy burden on protected speech."

Congress then passed the Child Online Protection Act (COPA) in 1998. Its provisions specifically singled out for prosecution only those who were "engaged in the business" of selling or distributing material deemed "harmful to minors"—that is, material considered obscene if viewed by minors, but not by adults. It also differed from the CDA in that only material on the World Wide Web was covered by the act, and not e-mail, newsgroups, Usenet, listservs, and other forms of Internet communication. The American Civil Liberties Union (ACLU) immediately challenged the constitutionality of COPA. A district court imposed an injunction on the implementation of the act, which was upheld by the Third Circuit Court of Appeals in June 2000.

While parents, the ACLU, and Congress agree that children must be protected from the threats posed by pornography, they disagree on the best way to do it. The authors in the following chapter debate whether pornography should be censored, and if so, how it can be done without violating the First Amendment.

"Censorship [should] be considered for the most violent and sexually explicit material now on offer."

Pornography Should Be Censored

Robert H. Bork

Robert H. Bork is a lawyer, law professor, former judge for the U.S. Court of Appeals, and author of *Slouching Towards Gomorrah: Modern Liberalism and American Decline*, from which this viewpoint is excerpted. Bork asserts that pornography is harmful to society and has no social value. Unless restrictions are placed on sexually explicit and violent material, American culture and society will degenerate into chaos. Furthermore, Bork contends, censorship is necessary to protect children from the effects of pornography.

As you read, consider the following questions:
1. What type of pornography is in demand on the Internet, according to Bork?
2. What is a pornographic culture, according to Angela Carter, as cited by the author?
3. According to Bork, how long has the United States practiced censorship?

Technology is now bringing worse material than we have ever seen or imagined, and, as technology develops further, the material will become still worse. The Internet now provides users access to what Simon Winchester calls "an untrammelled, uncontrolled, wholly liberated ocean of information." He thought it wonderful. Then one day he came upon a category called alt.sex, which has fifty-five groups including alt.sex.anal, alt.sex.intergen (intergenerational: the pedophile bulletin board), alt.sex.snuff (the killing of the victim) which includes subcategories for bestiality, torture, bloodletting, and sadistic injury.

Sexual Fantasies

The first category Winchester tried was alt.sex.stories, which contained a story about the kidnapping of two children. The castration of the 6-year-old boy is "reported in loving detail" and occurs before he is shot. The 7-year-old girl is then repeatedly raped by nine men before having her nipples cut off and her throat slashed. There were 200 such stories and the number was growing daily. "You want tales of fathers sodomizing their three-year-old daughters, or of mothers performing fellatio on their prepubescent sons, or of girls coupling with horses, or of the giving of enemas to child virgins? Then you need do no more than visit the newsgroup that is named 'alt.sex.stories' and all will reliably be there, 24 hours a day, for everyone with a computer and a telephone, anywhere on (or above) the face of the earth." The stories are written by pseudonymous authors and are filtered through two or three computers so that the authors and the points of origin are not known. The material is not only disgusting, it is a dangerous incitement. There is, for example: "A long and graphic account of exactly how and at what hour you wait outside a girls' school, how best to bundle a seven-year-old into your van, whether to tell her at the start of her ordeal that she is going to be killed at the end of it . . . how best to tie her down, which aperture to approach first, and with what—such things can only tempt those who verge on such acts to take a greater interest in them."

Users can download pornographic pictures as well as prose from the Internet. And there is a lot of both available.

The demand, moreover, is for material that can't be easily found elsewhere—pedophilia, sadomasochism, eroticized urination, defecation, and vaginal and rectal fisting. Among the most popular are sex acts with a wide variety of animals, nude children, and incest. The adult bulletin board service describes videos for sale and also provides over 25,000 pictures. The material is too obscene to be quoted here, but it involves girls defecating, girls eating feces (in both cases far more obscene language is used), oral sex with animals. One video is described as "Rape, torture, pussy nailed to table." It is impossible in short compass to give an adequate idea of the depravity that is being sold, apparently profitably.

The Internet, Stephen Bates informs us, offers plans for making bombs, instructions for painless suicide, the anti-Semitic forgery *Protocols of the Elders of Zion* (compressed for faster downloading), and racist diatribes, along with sexual perversion. There are certain to be offline harms from this material. "Pedophiles will abuse children they first met on-line, kids will blow off fingers with Net's bomb recipes, despondent teens will poison themselves using recipes from *alt.suicide.holiday*. Maybe all these tragedies would have occurred without the Net, but that's tough to prove." It would be even tougher to prove that this material has any social value. Only the most radical individualism imaginable could countenance these uses of the Internet.

What Winchester says of the alt.sex.stories he read is true of these other categories of prose and images: "Surely such essays tell the thinker of forbidden thoughts that there exists somewhere out there a like-minded group of men for whom such things are really not so bad, the enjoyment of which, if no one is so ill-starred as to get caught, can be limitless. Surely it is naive folly—or, the other end of the spectrum, gross irresponsibility—to suppose otherwise."

The Situation Will Worsen

But the situation is likely to get still worse than this. The pornographic video industry is now doing billions of dollars worth of business and volume is increasing rapidly. Companies are acquiring inventories of videos for cable television, and a nationwide chain of pornographic video retail stores is in the works. This may, however, be only a transitional phase. George Gilder predicts that computers will soon replace television, allowing viewers to call up digital films and files of whatever they may desire from around the world. He discounts the idea that "liberated children [will] rush away from the network nurse, chasing Pied Piper pederasts, snuff-film sadists, and other trolls of cyberspace." (The "network nurse," as a matter of fact, looks increasingly like a lady of the evening.) The computer will give everyone his own channel to do with as he wishes, and Gilder predicts a spectacular proliferation of programs on specialized cultural, scientific, and practical subjects.

That will certainly happen, but the presence of wholesome films and files does not rule out the presence of the corrupt and even diabolical. The Internet is proving that. The more private viewing becomes, the more likely it is that salacious and perverted tastes will be indulged. That proposition is demonstrated by the explosion of pornographic films and profits when videocassettes enabled customers to avoid the embarrassment of entering "adult" theaters. An even greater surge in the demand for perverted sex with violence will certainly occur when customers don't even have to check cassettes out of a store. Calling up films in their own homes, they will not have to face a clerk or let other customers see them browsing through x-rated films.

A Very Great Menace

When digital films become available for viewing on home computers, we are likely to discover that Gilder's "trolls of cyberspace" are very real, very popular, and a very great menace. Imagine Internet's alt.sex.stories on digital film available on home computers anywhere in the world. The dramatization, in living color with lurid special effects, of men castrating and then shooting a 6-year-old boy, then gang raping and killing a 7-year-old girl, is certain to trigger imitations by borderline perverts. Don't think such films won't be made; they will. Don't think that they will not be defended on First Amendment grounds; they will. And don't suppose it will not be said that the solution is simple: if you don't like it, don't watch it. That, too, will be argued.

A great many people are willing to deplore such material but unwilling to take or allow action to stop its distribution. When the Senate Commerce Committee approved a proposal to impose criminal penalties on anyone who transmits on Internet material that is "obscene, lewd, lascivious, filthy, or indecent," ferocious opposition immediately developed from a coalition of business and civil liberties organizations. The wording of the bill leaves much to be desired, but that is not the primary objection these groups have. They do not want restrictions, period, no matter how carefully drawn. The coalition includes, of course, the ACLU [American Civil Liberties Union] and the ubiquitous Time Warner, which John Leo has said is "associated one way or another with most of the high-profile, high-profit acts, black and white, that are pumping nihilism into the culture. . . . We are living through a cultural collapse, and major corporations are presiding over that collapse and grabbing everything they can on the way down."

Censorship and Values

If you think pornography and/or obscenity is a serious problem, you have to be for censorship. I will go even further and say that if you want to prevent pornography and/or obscenity from becoming a problem, you have to be for censorship. And lest there be any misunderstanding as to what I am saying, I will put it as bluntly as possible: If you care for the quality of life in our American democracy, then you have to be for censorship.

Irving Kristol, *Society*, September/October 1999.

We are still on the way down and they are still grabbing. I do not suppose for a moment that Time Warner would produce films of the material to be found on the Internet's alt.sex. Nor would any major entertainment corporation. Not today or tomorrow, but as we grow accustomed to brutal and perverted sex, inhibitions will be lowered still further. Some businesses will make such films and some civil libertarians will deplore them, adding, of course, that they should not be banned. In the absence of restraints of some sort, however, everything that can be imagined, and some things that can't, yet, will eventually be produced and shown.

Propaganda for Fornication

Reflecting on where we have come, Maggie Gallagher wrote: "Sex was remade in the image of Hugh Hefner; Eros demoted from a god to a buffoon. Over the last thirty years, America transformed itself into a pornographic culture." Gallagher accepted Angela Carter's definition, stated in somewhat more basic Anglo-Saxon, that pornography is basically propaganda for fornication, and offered a definition of her own: "[A] pornographic culture is not one in which pornographic materials are published and distributed. A pornographic culture is one which accepts the ideas about sex on which pornography is based."

That is quite right, as far as it goes, but our popular culture has gone far beyond propagandizing for fornication. That seems almost innocent nowadays. What America increasingly produces and distributes is now propaganda for every perversion and obscenity imaginable. If many of us accept the assumptions on which that is based, and apparently many do, then we are well on our way to an obscene culture. The upshot is that American popular culture is in a free fall, with the bottom not yet in sight. This is what the liberal view of human nature has brought us to. The idea that men are naturally rational, moral creatures without the need for strong external restraints has been exploded by experience. There is an eager and growing market for depravity, and profitable industries devoted to supplying it. Much of such resistance as there is comes from people living on the moral capital accumulated by prior generations. That capital may be expected to dwindle further—cultures do not unravel everywhere all at once. Unless there is vigorous counterattack, which must, I think, resort to legal as well as moral sanctions, the prospects are for a chaotic and unhappy society, followed, perhaps, by an authoritarian and unhappy society.

The question is whether we are really content to accept that. . . .

Censorship Is Not Unthinkable

Sooner or later censorship is going to have to be considered as popular culture continues plunging to ever more sickening lows. The alternative to censorship, legal and moral, will be a brutalized and chaotic culture, with all that that entails for our society, economy, politics, and physical safety. It is important to be clear about the topic. I am *not* suggesting that censorship should, or constitutionally could, be employed to counter the liberal political and cultural propagandizing of movies, television, network news, and music. They are protected, and properly so, by the First Amendment's guarantees of freedom of speech and of the press. I *am* suggesting that censorship be considered for the most violent and sexually explicit material now on offer, starting with the obscene prose and pictures available on the Internet, motion pictures that are mere rhapsodies to violence, and the more degenerate lyrics of rap music. . . .

Is censorship really as unthinkable as we all seem to assume? That it is unthinkable is a very recent conceit. From the earliest colonies on this continent over 300 years ago, and for about 175 years of our existence as a nation, we endorsed and lived with censorship. We do not have to imagine what censorship might be like; we know from experience. Some of it was formal, written in statutes or city ordinances; some of it was informal, as in the movie producers' agreement to abide by the rulings of the Hayes Office. [The Hayes Office acted as an in-house censor for Hollywood movies during the first half of the twentieth century.] Some of it was inevitably silly—the rule that the movies could not show even a husband and wife fully dressed on a bed unless each had one foot on the floor—and some of it was no doubt pernicious. The period of Hayes office censorship was also, perhaps not coincidentally, the golden age of the movies. . . .

The debate about censorship, insofar as there can be said to be a debate, usually centers on the issue of keeping children away from pornography. There is, of course, a good deal of merit to that, but it makes the issue sound like one of child rearing, which most people would like the government to butt out of. Opponents say parents can protect their children by using control features offered by many services. Both sides are missing a major point. Aside from the fact that many parents will not use control features, censorship is also crucial to protect children—and the rest of us—from men encouraged to act by a steady diet of computerized pedophilia, murder, rape, and sado-masochism. No one supposes that every addict of such material will act out his fantasies, but it is willfully blind to think that none will. The pleasures the viewers of such material get from watching a thousand rape scenes or child kidnappings is not worth one actual rape or kidnapping.

"Most censors don't stop at what offends them . . . their overheated imaginations begin conjuring up what might offend this person or that group, and pretty soon everything is 'pornographic.'"

Pornography Should Not Be Censored

Peter McWilliams

In the following viewpoint, Peter McWilliams examines the arguments used to support censorship and asserts that it is frequently used to protect political or religious beliefs. However, since people do not always share the same beliefs, what may offend one person may not be offensive to someone else. For that reason, McWilliams maintains, deciding whether sexually explicit material is pornographic or not depends on the context and personal taste. McWilliams is the author of *Ain't Nobody's Business If You Do*, from which this viewpoint is excerpted.

As you read, consider the following questions:
1. What are the three basic subjects of censorship, according to McWilliams?
2. In the author's view, what is the problem with pornography?
3. What does censorship ultimately come down to, in the author's opinion?

C ensorship applies to basically three subjects: (1) Sex, (2) Violence, and (3) Ideas. Of the three, censorship of ideas is by far the most serious. It is also, by far, the most subtle.

Mothers Behind Censorship

A major motivation behind censorship is *paternalism.* "You are not able to deal with this information," the censor says; "therefore—for your own protection—we will keep it from you." The variation on that, of course, is "*You and I* will not be corrupted by this, but *they*—those poor uneducated, unsophisticated, unwashed masses—will not be able to handle it, so, for their own good and the good of society, we'll ban it."

The other major motivation—far more pernicious—is to *protect power.* Here, someone or some group with power decides, "If this information got out, it might prove damaging to my (our) power, so I'd (we'd) better suppress it." What usually follows that statement is a long list of justifications—if the justifications didn't precede it—which generally run along the lines of, "It's not true anyway," "This is distorted and will confuse people," "The people saying this have ulterior motives," "This is inflammatory," "This is un-American," and so on.

All censorship is a violation of the First Amendment:

> Congress shall make no law respecting an establishment of religion, or prohibiting the free exercise thereof; or abridging the freedom of speech, or of the press; or the right of the people peaceably to assemble, and to petition the Government for a redress of grievances.

It was a brilliant move for the founding fathers to put all of these guarantees together in one amendment. Almost all censorship is based on the religious and/or political beliefs of those in power. The bottom-line justification for censorship is invariably (a) "It's immoral!" (meaning, of course, against their religious beliefs), and/or (b) "It's un-American!" (which means it doesn't agree with their view about the kind of government America should have and the way that government should be run). Most censorship violates our First Amendment rights to (a) freedom of and from religion and (b) "petition the government for a redress of grievances." Even if the "freedom of speech, or of the press" clause were not there, applying the remainder of the First Amendment would eliminate almost all censorship as we know it.

"Clear and Present Danger"

But just in case the primary justification for all censorship—that is, religious and political suppression—was missed, the founding fathers added the freedom of speech and press clause: "Congress shall make no law . . . abridging the freedom of speech, or of the press." As I've asked before, what could be clearer than that? The only limitation on this freedom is, as always, directly threatening the person or property of innocent people with physical harm. Supreme Court Justice Oliver Wendell Holmes expressed this in his famous example from 1919:

> The most stringent protection of free speech would not protect a man in falsely shouting fire in a theatre and causing a panic. [The] question in every case is whether the words used are used in such circumstances and are of such a nature as to create a clear and present danger that they will bring about the substantive evils that Congress has a right to prevent.

One could not, then, in supervising the demolition of a building, give the order, "Blow it up," knowing that there still were people inside. The willful murder of those people cannot be protected by saying, "Well, I was just exercising my right of free speech." Unfortunately, over the years, the "clear and present danger" of "substantive evils" that Justice Holmes gave as exceptions to the First Amendment rights has been interpreted beyond his obvious physical example of knowingly starting a panic in a public theater by yelling "Fire!" The "clear and present danger" has been interpreted as a potential danger to our national *morality*—and we've already established the source of most "morality."

In 1991, for example, the Supreme Court ruled that nude dancing by women in a Las Vegas bar was *not* protected by the First Amendment. This dancing, the Court held, was on the level of shouting "Fire!" in a crowded theater. How far *backward* we have gone from '19 to '91. This is considered a landmark decision. As Stanford University law professor Gerald Gunther explained, "The court is saying that public morality trumps legitimate rights of expression. That's never happened before."

In the past, one had to define the "clear and present danger" by comparing whether or not the censored material would potentially cause the same physical harm as shouting, "Fire!" in a crowded theater. Now, the "clear and present danger" need only be as potentially harmful as consenting adults dancing nude in front of other consenting adults, in a bar—*in Las Vegas*. What a wonderful gift the Supreme Court gave us in 1991 to celebrate the 200th anniversary of the passage of the Bill of Rights. . . .

With censorship, we find another conservative-liberal division over which activity justifies "bending" the First Amendment. When either side wants to censor, conservatives usually want to censor the sexual; liberals generally want to censor violence. Neither camp uses the word *censor*—they use words such as *curb, protect, control, modify, limit*, and so on.

Might I remind both camps that *any* "abridging" is a violation of the First Amendment?

The Problem with Pornography

The problem with pornography is that it is done so *poorly*. "There is no such thing as a moral or an immoral book," said Oscar Wilde more than one hundred years ago. "Books are well written, or badly written. That is all." Nothing much has changed since then. In 1993, Calvin Tomkins wrote in the *New Yorker*:

> Of all the minor art forms, pornography has remained the least developed. Certified pornographic masterworks, from Sappho to Nabokov, can be counted on the fingers of one hand. The best-known critical theorists of the form, from Anthony Comstock to Jesse Helms, have had the disadvantage of being morons. The National Endowment for the Arts supports pornographic experiment unwillingly, at best, and our popular culture contents itself with unimaginative increases in the gross annual depiction of bare skin and earnest copulation.

Violence has its artists—Sam Peckinpah, Francis Ford Coppola, Ridley Scott. Where are pornography's artists? Twenty years ago, *Deep Throat* got publicity just because it had *a plot*. What have we got today? Mapplethorpe and Madonna?

Once upon a time, some of our best artists gave us our erotica. Today the Bible is used as a reason to censor. Not long ago, it was used as a method to *avoid* the censor. Michelangelo was able to do a magnificent male nude statue by calling it "David" (the model's real name was probably something closer to Tadzio). Michelangelo was also able to place a reclining male nude in the very center of the ceiling of the Sistine Chapel (the pope's personal chapel, for heaven's sake) by calling it "Adam."

The Regulation of Pornography

Let us assume for a moment that most sexually explicit materials were crude, demeaning of the sacred aspects of human sexuality, advocating values inconsistent with the values central to our society, and simply poor quality communication, *but a small percentage were the opposite.* We dare not censor, control or restrict access to all such materials because of the failings of some or even most. Government is uniquely ill-equipped to make determinations as to what is "good" or "high quality" communication. Governmental decisions about communication necessarily will be biased towards non-controversial material. Furthermore, censorship based on sexual content will necessarily eliminate the material which makes serious social contributions, especially if the audience for that material is outside the perceived social mainstream.

Jeffrey J. Douglas, testimony before the Subcommittee on Telecommunications, Trade, and Consumer Protection, September 11, 1998.

Gustave Doré (1832–1883), who had a taste for subjects not acceptable in his own time (although his obvious love for sex and violence would be right at home in our time), was able to create some of the most bizarre art of the nineteenth century simply by illustrating Bible stories. Because he had the good sense to call his etchings, "The Deluge" and "Jehu's Companions Finding the Remains of Jezebel," his work was welcomed in the same Victorian parlors and praised by the same Victorian social leaders who probably would have put him in jail if he had accurately entitled his etchings, "Naked Man, Naked Woman, and Four Naked Children Writhing in the Water and on a Wet Rock" and "Selected Body Parts of an Attractive Young Woman Being Examined by Four Men Prior to Being Eaten by Dogs." Because he was clever, however, *Doré's Bible* became so popular many people assumed that he wrote the text, too.

"I don't think pornography is very harmful," Sir Noel Coward summed it up in 1972, "but it is terribly, terribly boring."

Presidential Commissions Study Pornography

In 1967, Congress established and funded a National Commission on Pornography. Its report, published in 1970, found that it was not *pornography*, but the puritanical attitudes *toward* pornography that cause problems in America. The report said the problems stemmed "from the inability or reluctance of people in our society to be open and direct in dealing with sexual matters." In surveys, the commission found that only 2% of Americans thought sexually explicit material was a significant social problem. The report recommended that all legislation interfering with the right of adults to read, obtain, or view explicit sexual material be repealed.

The findings of this exhaustive study did not happen to fit the personal morals of Washington's power structure—from President Nixon on down. Nothing was done about repealing the laws.

When President Reagan put together another commission to study pornography, he did it *right*—*extreme* right. Attorney General Edwin Meese carefully selected eleven God-fearing (and, apparently, *sex-fearing*) Americans. One of the Meese Commission members was James C. Dobson, who wrote:

> That is what the pornographers are doing to my country. They are hammering down the supporting columns and blasting away the foundations. We must stop the devastation before the entire superstructure crashes to the earth! With the diligent prayers and personal involvement of God-fearing people, we can save the great edifice called America. But there is not a minute to lose. "But each one is tempted when he is carried away and enticed by his own lust. Then when lust has conceived, it gives birth to sin; and when sin is accomplished, it brings forth death."
>
> (James 1:14–16, NASB) [italics in original]

Is there any doubt where his personal sense of morality comes from? And does the rhetoric sound familiar? It is part of what Donna A. Demac, in her book, *Liberty Denied: The Current Rise of Censorship in America*, calls (quoting Hugh Hefner) "sexual McCarthyism":

The antipornography movement of the 1980s represents yet another attempt by certain groups to impose their morals on the rest of society. What makes these efforts more threatening than those of the past is the extent to which they have been abetted by federal, state, and local authorities. The climate engendered by initiatives such as the Meese Commission has been described with only a bit of hyperbole by Hugh Hefner as "sexual McCarthyism."

The Problem with Censorship

. . . The problem with censorship can be summed up in two words: *who decides?*

If someone other than the end consumers—voting with their purchases, attendance, or remote controls—decides what should or should not, can or cannot, must or must not be said, depicted, or offered for sale, who should that person be? And who decides who that person should be? And who decides if those people are doing a good job deciding? Ultimately, censorship comes down to *taste*. What offends me may enlighten you. Do you want *me* deciding—based on my taste and construct of morality—what *you* should or should not be exposed to?

Most censors don't stop at what offends them, of course: their overheated imaginations begin conjuring up what might offend this person or that group, and pretty soon *everything* is "pornographic." Many start sounding like Mervyn Griffiths-Jones, the prosecuting attorney in the 1960 trial to keep *Lady Chatterly's Lover* banned:

> You may think one of the ways in which you can test this book is to ask yourself the question: would you approve of your own son and daughter, because girls can read as well as boys, reading this book? Is it a book you could have lying in your own house? Is it a book you would wish your wife or your servant to read?

So much of what we'd want to censor depends on where we stand, what we're standing on, and whom we're standing with—rather than simply what we can't stand. Shelley Winters, tongue well in cheek, pointed out,

> I think nudity on the stage is disgusting, shameful and unpatriotic. But if I were twenty-two with a great body, it would be artistic, tasteful, patriotic and a progressive, religious experience.

In addition, besides deciding what's good and what's bad, who decides what the punishment should be for violating these standards? For example, consider this comment from a young artist: "Anybody who sees and paints a sky green and pastures blue ought to be sterilized."

This may seem to be a trivial, even silly, comment for a young artist to make, but what if this young artist sets aside his art and turns to the art of politics? What if he gains enough power to fulfill not only his censorship dreams, but to inflict the punishments he finds appropriate? Well, that's precisely what happened. The artist-turned-politician who detested green skies and blue pastures had tens of thousands sterilized, and presided over the most sterile artistic period in the history of Europe—and these were the least of his crimes. As I'm sure you've guessed, the censor was Adolph Hitler. . . .

"I was arrested for using a ten-letter word that began with 'c,'" said Lenny Bruce, "and I would marry no woman who was not one." From the standpoint of consensual crimes and freedom of speech, (if I may paraphrase Lenny Bruce) we must use that marvelous ten-letter word that begins with "t" (and certainly no one would marry me who didn't have a great deal of it): *toleration*. If I don't want Jerry Falwell editing my books, I must forgo the luxury of editing his sermons. (But I can dream, can't I?) To have a freedom ourselves, we must pick up the banner of that great light of the Enlightenment, Voltaire, and declare: "I disapprove of what you say, but I will defend to the death your right to say it."

As long as we keep censoring things, we are lost in the *symptoms* of our society's problems, thus ignoring the problems themselves. Pornography, for example, doesn't degrade women; women are degraded by our culture, and certain forms of pornography reflect that. Yes, we have a serious problem with the way women are treated in our culture, and pornography is a symptom, but let's not kill the messenger. Let's get the message and *do something about it*.

"The [Supreme] Court reaffirmed that 'the Government has an interest in protecting children from potentially harmful materials.'"

The Federal Government Can Regulate Internet Pornography

Dan Coats

In the following viewpoint, Dan Coats, a senator from Indiana, testifies before the U.S. House Commerce Committee's Subcommittee on Telecommunications, Trade, and Consumer Protection about the need for a law that would require purveyors of Internet pornography to bar minors from access to their websites. Coats argues that the bill he favors, known as the Child Online Protection Act, is constitutional because it regulates only obscene material that is commercially available on the Internet and is harmful to minors. In addition, Coats refutes the claim that Internet porn laws are unenforceable by pointing out that current technology ensures that Internet porn sites can verify the age of their users. The bill was signed into law by Bill Clinton in October 1998, but was immediately challenged in court. An injunction has prevented the bill from being implemented.

As you read, consider the following questions:
1. What are the three requirements of a "harmful to minors" test, as cited by the author?
2. Why do so few minors possess a credit card, according to Coats?

Excerpted from Dan Coats's testimony before the U.S. House Commerce Committee, Subcommittee on Telecommunications, Trade, and Consumer Protection, September 11, 1998.

I would like to begin by thanking the distinguished Chairman and Members of the Committee for providing me the opportunity to appear before you today.

On November 8 of last year (1997), I introduced S.1482. This legislation is designed to require commercial pornographers on the Web to restrict access by minors to pornographic material. Subsequently, Congressmen Michael Oxley and James Greenwood, on April 30 of this year (1998), introduced the counterpart legislation that will be discussed today. This legislative effort is a product of the Supreme Court ruling in *Reno v. ACLU* [which struck] down the "indecency" provisions of the Communications Decency Act or CDA [a 1996 law designed to regulate Internet pornography]. The bill requires that commercial pornographers on the Web take certain steps designed to restrict access by children to pornographic material. Fines and penalties under the legislation are identical to those imposed under the dial-a-porn laws.

Internet Pornography Can Be Regulated

It is first important to note that the Court did not strike down the entire CDA. Rather, the Court struck down the "indecent" and "patently offensive" sections of the CDA. For example, the obscenity provisions of the Act were not challenged and remain good law today. This is significant in the face of false arguments claiming that the Court established that pornographic material on the Internet cannot be regulated. It can, and is.

In fact, at the outset of its ruling in *Reno* the Court reaffirmed that "the Government has an interest in protecting children from potentially harmful materials," and acknowledged "the Act's legitimate purposes."

It is this compelling Government interest, and legitimate purpose that this legislation seeks to address. The bill is carefully tailored to conform with the concerns outlined in the Court's ruling in the CDA.

The "harmful to minors" standard adopted in this legislation was first upheld by the Supreme Court in *Ginsberg v. New York*. The New York statute prohibited the selling to minors under 17 years of age material that was considered obscene to them even if not obscene to adults. . . .

Four Differences

The Supreme Court found four primary differences between the CDA and the statute upheld in *Ginsberg*. First, the Court pointed out that in *Ginsberg* "the prohibition against sales to minors does not bar parents who desire from purchasing the magazines for their children." This legislation in no way prohibits parents from taking such action.

"Second, the New York statute applied only to commercial transactions."

Again, the scope of this legislation is strictly limited to commercial transactions. The operative term in the bill is "engaged in the business" . . . [of] trafficking of obscene material.

The Court also pointed out in *Reno* the New York statute upheld in the *Ginsberg* decision combined its definition with the requirement that the material be without "social importance to minors" and that the material "lack serious literary, artistic, political, or scientific value."

By adopting the construction followed in the New York statute these concerns are directly addressed. This ensures that the bill may not be construed as to restrict access to public health information, important works of art, literature, and political information.

The "harmful to minors" standard is a three-prong test. It requires that the material appeal to the prurient interest, that it be patently offensive as to what is suitable to minors and that—taken as a whole—it lack any serious literary, artistic, political, or scientific value as to minors. All three prongs must be met for the material to be determined harmful to minors.

"Fourth, the New York statute defined a minor as a person under the age of 17." Our legislation adopts the same "under the age of 17" requirement.

Thus, each concern regarding the content standard outlined by the Court in the *Reno* is specifically addressed under this legislative approach.

Credit Cards and Feasibility

The use of credit cards, access codes and PIN numbers is standard technology for commercial activity on the Web. The Court acknowledged as much stating: "Technology exists by which an operator of a Web site may condition access on the verification of requested information such as a credit card or an adult password." Further, the Court stated: "Although such verification is actually being used by some commercial providers of sexually explicit material, the District Court's findings indicate that it is not economically feasible for most non-commercial speakers."

Again, in a direct response to the Court's concerns, the legislation is strictly limited to the Web, where the Court established technological feasibility, and to commercial Web sites where the Court established economic feasibility.

In fact, regarding this economic feasibility question, Adult Verification Services, or AVSs, generally provide their services free of charge to Web site operators, even providing a kick-back to site operators for customers referred to them. Therefore, it is not only economically feasible, but often profitable to use an AVS service.

MIDNIGHT IN THE GARDEN OF GOOD AND EVIL

Jim Borgman. Reprinted by special permission of King Features Syndicate.

Though credit cards likely will continue to be the most widely used access restriction measure, AVS services provide for other means of verification and payment for adults who do not possess a credit card. As to the effectiveness of credit cards, though there are no laws specifically requiring that minors not be issued credit cards, the use of credit cards fall under state contract law to the extent that a contract entered into by a minor is unenforceable. Most states define minors as those under 18 (some may use 21).

The practical effect of this is rare access to credit cards by those under 18. Even then, under this legislation, the commercial operator is not held liable for the industrious minor who succeeds in defeating any of the proscribed access restriction measures. Rather, they enjoy a defense from prosecution simply by having the access restriction measures in place.

Another argument for those who would defeat efforts to protect children from on-line smut is that the Internet is a global medium that defies regulation and enforcement. On this point, we need look no further than the headlines of the story of a multi-national crackdown on an on-line child pornography ring. The details of this successful law enforcement effort point to the hollowness of the "unenforceable" argument.

In summary, the Oxley/Greenwood bill, introduced as a companion to my Senate bill, is a carefully crafted response to the Supreme Court's ruling in *Reno v. ACLU*.

Teachers' Concerns

I would like to read from a letter sent to me by a group of teachers and administrators at South Knox High School in Southern Indiana:

Senator Coats,

We are writing to express our concerns about the use of the Internet by America's children. We are all in agreement that the Internet is a technology that is, and will be, of enormous benefit in our classrooms. However, our concerns are with the magnitude of pornography on the Internet, and our inability to protect our students as we struggle to keep up with technology and to place computers in all of our classrooms.

In our school, students must be supervised by a teacher while using the Internet. But, as we move the Internet from the library into our teaching classrooms, constant supervision will not always be possible.

The school where we work and teach has two security blocks

on our Internet system. We use both Cyber Patrol and Fortress. What we now know is that there is no blocking system available to us today that is adequate. We have one person in charge of the computer system in our school system who could work full-time just blocking pornography that teachers and students have found and reported.

We are all working hard to make it possible for the students at South Knox High School, a small rural school, to have Internet exposure. Yet, Senator, how are we supposed to know that if you type in Fiesta on the Internet, you may get a bare chested woman posing in a suggestive manner? We have seen pictures on the Internet in our school library of a man and woman participating in oral sex. We have also seen tattooed penises and testicles. If a child wants to look up a type of doll that she has, she can type in water baby. One of her choices is a site with pictures of adult women, naked except for a wet diaper, or a woman pictured from behind, urinating in her underpants.

We spend 180 days, eight hours a day, five days a week caring for and educating America's children. We must have a safeguard that works for the Internet, during school hours, so that we may keep up with the world yet not have our children innocently exposed to pornography.

Take Responsibility

Sometime in the next few weeks Congress will consider legislation that would establish a moratorium on Internet taxation. I, like so many Members of this Committee, generally support this effort. However, I think that it would be a sad day indeed if Congress acted to provide a tax shelter for commercial porn sites on the Web without first requiring them to take responsible measures to protect children from exposure to the smut they peddle for profit.

"Speech that is appropriate for adults, . . . may not be appropriate for young children— nevertheless, the Internet cannot be limited to what is only appropriate for them."

Federal Regulation of Internet Pornography Is Unconstitutional

Charles Levendosky

Charles Levendosky is the editor of the *Casper (Wyoming) Star-Tribune* and a noted commentator on First Amendment issues. In the following viewpoint, Levendosky argues that the Child Online Protection Act (COPA)—a law passed by Congress in late 1998 to prevent children from being exposed to pornography online—is unconstitutional. The First Amendment prohibits Congress from passing any law censoring free speech, and yet, Levendosky maintains, this is exactly what COPA does. Furthermore, he contends that limiting the Internet only to material that does not offend children places an unacceptable limit on free speech. An injunction against the COPA was upheld by the Third Circuit Court of Appeals in June 2000.

As you read, consider the following questions:
1. What law regulating online pornography was struck down by the Supreme Court in 1997, according to the author?
2. What is the three-pronged test for whether Internet material is considered "harmful to minors," as cited by Levendosky?

Reprinted, with permission, from "New Internet Censorship Law Will Fail," by Charles Levendosky, *Casper Star-Tribune*, January 17, 1999.

Congress passed another unconstitutional piece of legislation in 1998 and attached it as a rider to the 40-pound, 4,000-page Omnibus Appropriations Bill. When President Bill Clinton signed the bill into law, the Internet censorship act became law, too—bad law.

The Child Online Protection Act

Once again, members of Congress ignored the First Amendment's proscription: "Congress shall make no law . . . abridging the freedom of speech," and passed the Child Online Protection Act (COPA). The law contains the same constitutional problems that were found in the Communications Decency Act, which was struck down by a unanimous vote of the U.S. Supreme Court in 1997.

In the guise of protecting children from online smut, Congress created a new federal crime. Anyone who knowingly makes material that is "harmful to minors" available on the World Wide Web for commercial purposes can be fined $50,000 and spend up to six months in jail—for each violation. Worse, a person can be fined $50,000 for each day that such material was made available.

According to COPA, "The term 'minor' means any person under 17 years of age." And the term "commercial purposes" is broad enough to include anyone using the Internet to gather or post information while conducting research that might lead to publication.

COPA defines "harmful to minors" as any material that is obscene, which is already illegal. However, "harmful to minors" also includes 1) material that the average person would find appeals to a minor's prurient interest; 2) depicts sex acts in a manner that is patently offensive to minors; and 3) "taken as a whole lacks serious literary, artistic, political, or scientific value for minors." All three conditions must be met before material can be considered "harmful to minors."

Those familiar with First Amendment case law will recognize this three-prong test as a variation on the Miller test from the U.S. Supreme Court's decision in *Miller v. California* (1973). The courts use the Miller test to determine whether a book, movie, video or other material is obscene.

The problem here, however, is that an adult must guess

what is patently offensive to a minor and what would appeal to a minor's prurient interest and what would lack serious literary value for a minor.

For most 15-year-old boys, almost any material that hints at sex, even bra ads in the Sears catalogue, would appeal to their prurient interest. And one could argue that it would be nearly impossible to find sexual material that would be patently offensive to boys that age.

Would special prosecutor Kenneth Starr's report, which details the sex acts that Clinton and Monica Lewinsky allegedly committed, be harmful to minors? Would Starr's report have political value for a 16-year-old? Probably. But what about an 8-year-old?

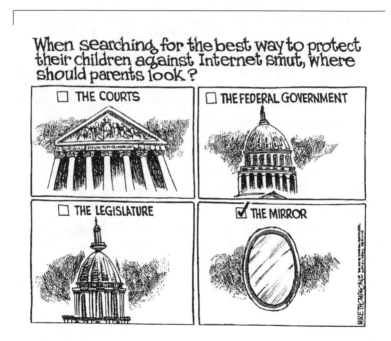

Mike Thompson. Reprinted by permission of Copley News Service.

Yet Congress considered the report important enough to post on the World Wide Web—and rightfully so. Whether or not the public agrees with Starr's allegations or the manner in which they were described, the report is politically and historically significant as part of the Republican Party's attempt to remove a Democratic president from office.

The crux of the problem, then—should law-abiding citizens only post material on the Internet that would not offend or "harm" an 8-year-old?

When COPA Falls Short

And that is precisely where COPA falls short. Speech that is appropriate for adults, like a discussion of rapes in prison or genital mutilation, may not be appropriate for young children—nevertheless, the Internet cannot be limited to what is only appropriate for them.

In the Supreme Court's 1997 decision concerning the constitutionality of the Communications Decency Act, Justice John Paul Stevens wrote: "In order to deny minors access to potentially harmful speech, the CDA effectively suppresses a large amount of speech that adults have a constitutional right to receive and to address to one another. That burden on adult speech is unacceptable if less restrictive alternatives would be at least as effective in achieving the legitimate purpose that the statute was enacted to serve." The high court has made this exact point in numerous cases before 1997.

Acting Assistant Attorney General L. Anthony Sutin of the U.S. Department of Justice sent a letter to the House Committee on Commerce to spell out the department's objections to COPA. Sutin wrote that attempting to enforce the provisions of the act would divert "investigative and prosecutorial resources that the Department currently invests in combating traffickers of hard-core pornography, in thwarting child predators, and in prosecuting large-scale and multi district commercial distributors of obscene materials." Sutin also noted that COPA has serious constitutional flaws.

It's axiomatic that when a law attempts to restrict constitutionally protected speech based upon its content, the law violates the First Amendment. Somehow, members of Congress fail to understand this nation's long and honorable freedom of speech tradition.

COPA sweeps too broadly and too vaguely to be constitutional. And it does not take the least restrictive means to achieve its worthy goal of protecting children from speech they might find shocking or disturbing—and that is reason enough to toss this act into the junk-pile of history.

The act requires anyone who has a Web site that contains sexual material to verify the age of those who want to view the site. Age verification technologies are prohibitively expensive. The requirement would shut down many, if not most, educational Web sites.

The American Civil Liberties Union and 16 other plaintiffs challenged COPA the day after it was signed into law. Judge Lowell A. Reed Jr. of the Federal District Court in Philadelphia granted a temporary restraining order that prohibits enforcement of the act until Feb. 1, 1999. The judge noted that it is likely the ACLU would prevail on the merits of some of their claims. [The Third Circuit Court of Appeals upheld the injunction in June 2000.]

If this case reaches the Supreme Court, we can expect the law to be overturned with a finality that will strengthen free speech law as it applies to the Internet. And that result will be well worth the time and resources spent defending our First Amendment rights.

"[An] advantage of an adult domain . . . is that it would aid in shielding children from the large amount of unprosecuted obscenity already present in U.S. web sites on the Internet."

Internet Pornography Should Have Its Own Domain

Bruce Watson

Bruce Watson is the president of Enough Is Enough, an organization that works to educate the public about the dangers of online pornography. The following viewpoint is from Watson's testimony before the Child Online Protection Act (COPA) Commission, which was researching ways to restrict children's access to pornography on the Internet. Watson contends that one way to shield minors from pornography is to establish a separate domain name, such as ".sex" or ".adult," for pornographic websites. A mandatory, separate domain name would make it easier for software filters to detect online pornography and for parents to protect their children.

As you read, consider the following questions:
1. What two words are among the most commonly used terms entered into search engines, according to Watson?
2. Which country prosecuted an operator of a porn website who located the site overseas to escape jurisdiction, as cited by the author?
3. How many cases of Internet obscenity has the Justice Department prosecuted in the last five years, according to Watson?

Excerpted from Bruce Watson's testimony before the Child Online Protection Act Commission, Washington, D.C., June 8, 2000.

Thank you for the opportunity to speak today in support of a separate Internet domain for material that is harmful to minors. At Enough Is Enough, we believe that such a domain can be an important part of the solution to child protection online.

Let me be clear, however, that we are not suggesting that such a domain is a "silver bullet" that would render all other parts of the solution unnecessary. The Internet is probably the most significant revolution in communications since the invention of the printing press. It would be simplistic to imagine that the issues it raises could be solved by any single panacea.

The Role of Parents

The most commonly suggested single panacea (in some quarters) is that child protection online should be left entirely to parents. Parents certainly have the primary responsibility for raising their children, and their responsibility is no less in the area of Internet safety. However, it is simply unrealistic to believe that parents can do the job alone—even if they were as Internet-literate as their children, which is frequently not the case.

By comparison, parents also have the primary responsibility to teach their children about the dangers of irresponsible use of tobacco or alcohol. But in those areas (where, incidentally, many parents have more knowledge than they do about the Internet) parents also have the support of laws making it illegal for others to provide alcohol or tobacco to their children—not to mention restrictions on even advertising such products to minors.

We believe that children's protection online similarly requires separate but complimentary responsibilities on the part of parents; other gatekeepers like teachers and librarians; the internet industry; the law and law enforcement; and, yes, maybe even the pornographers too. A separate domain would be an assist to meet these various responsibilities, not an opiate to make them go away.

An adult zone will make HtM material much easier to isolate.

There is a considerable amount of misinformation and disinformation about filtering. Opponents of filtering trumpet any examples of over- or under-blocking with a glee that dramatically overstates their frequency, and sometimes suggest that all filters depend on simple word association, which is simply not true.

Nevertheless, it is certainly true that identifying all new porn sites is a significant challenge for filtering companies, whether their software operates by some form of artificial intelligence or by using so-called "spiders" to add to their proprietary database. With an adult domain, however, filtering a large portion of the troublesome material becomes instead a binary question—a "yes or no" test.

The advantage of this binary test would be to make it significantly easier to protect children from HtM material. How difficult would it be, for example, for AOL and other service providers to add "block adult domain" to their list of parental control options? The same question could presumably be added to any browser.

A Broad-Based Solution

A broad based problem needs a broad based solution.

The Internet, for all its many blessings, has also created an unprecedented, effortless and almost automatic distribution system for pornographers. It is no exaggeration to point out that it is easier for a 12-year-old to find hard-core pornography on the Internet today, than it was for an adult to find it in many American cities ten years ago. (By "hardcore" I mean what prosecutors call "penetration clearly visible," or PCV, not mere *Playboy* centerfolds.) By comparison with this effortless distribution system, solutions like filtering software and one-click-away resources require effort and expertise on the parts of parents.

While we support "one-click-away" solutions—in fact, three years ago our own website was one of the first to provide this type of help—we also recognize that, compared to the effortless reach of the distribution system, such solutions have a limited audience. Part of the solution, at least, must be coextensive with the reach of the problem—just as the limitations on selling or advertising tobacco or alcohol apply to all minors, not just those whose parents best understand the problem.

Zoning is what we already do in the physical world.

The right objective for Cyberspace with respect to HtM

material should be for it to be subject to the same standards as the physical world—neither more nor less. Our society accepts that certain material is acceptable for adults but not for kids; as illustrated, for example, by the zoning of sexually oriented businesses that are for adults only, or the use of blinder racks for adult magazines in newsstands. A "dot adult" Internet zone recognizes the same reality. Why would we *not* apply the same concept to cyberspace?

Questions and Answers

Would an adult domain create an attractive nuisance that would make it easier for children to find HtM materials?

Unfortunately, lest we forget, it would be just about impossible for pornography to be easier to find on the Internet than it already is. . . . If a person is looking for pornography on the Internet, it is already almost impossible to miss.

The words "sex" and "porn" are consistently at or near the top of the list of words entered into search engines, and lead quickly to free samples of hard-core material. In other words, the attractive nuisance already exists. With an adult domain, however, the attractive nuisance would at least be easier to isolate.

A Good Idea

Some Internet-based pornographers . . . have been calling for a domain of their own. They say it would be good for business.

That's just fine. If those who proffer obscenity want to house it in a red-light district, so much the easier for people like me to avoid it.

Melana Zyla, *USA Today*, April 8, 1998.

If U.S. law required use of the domain, would this lead HtM sites to move offshore?

The answer to this question has a number of parts. Firstly, if a U.S. corporation or individual placed a porn web site offshore, it is not self-evident that they would necessarily escape U.S. jurisdiction—any more than the person who opens an offshore bank account necessarily avoids Internal Revenue Service (IRS) jurisdiction over the interest income. It is interesting to note that England has already prosecuted an English porn site operator who located his site here in the U.S. in the vain hope of escaping English jurisdiction.

Secondly, the U.S. is not the only country troubled by this issue, which is under serious study with varying legislative proposals in the European Union, Australia and other countries. Between shared concerns and moral suasion, the number of potential havens could be expected to drop with the passage of time. Already, in the battle against child pornography, there is a notable amount of international cooperation—for example, the roundup of the "Wonderland" child pornography ring, which involved simultaneous arrests in twelve countries.

The U.S. has been the leader in developing the Internet. Should we not also be the leader in developing solutions to the problems it has brought with it?

Would creating an adult domain effectively legalize obscenity?

Creating an adult domain for HtM material would not legitimize obscenity any more than creating a sexually-oriented business zone does in the physical world. In neither case does the decision to create an adult zone imply that obscene materials will be or should be free from prosecution.

Another advantage of an adult domain, however, is that it would aid in shielding children from the large amount of unprosecuted obscenity already present in U.S. web sites on the Internet. At a public hearing of the House Commerce Committee here in Washington, representatives of the Justice Department confirmed—albeit grudgingly—that they have initiated almost no prosecutions of Internet obscenity in the last five years. While this lack of energy by the Justice Department is a scandal in itself, an adult domain would at least provide some level of safety net between children and any unprosecuted obscenity on the Internet.

Inclusion in Adult Domain Sites

Should it be mandatory for porn sites to reside in the adult domain?

In an ideal world, it would not be necessary to make compliance mandatory. In fact, ideally porn sites would already have taken voluntary steps to keep their materials from younger eyes. Instead, however, we find the opposite— "stealth" porn sites using child-appeal brand names like Disney, Pokemon, or Barbie to bring traffic to their sites. It is obviously unlikely that the owners of such sites would voluntarily relocate to an adult domain, since, for whatever reason, advertising to children appears already to be part of their standard operating procedure. The use of an adult domain by HtM sites should, therefore, be made mandatory.

Is it possible to adequately define which materials should be in this domain?

It's interesting that this question causes more trouble to well-meaning academics than it does to commercial pornographers, who know exactly what will sell—and it's not Michelangelo's *David* or AIDS prevention information. The guy running the Pink Kitty Porn Palace isn't showing video tours of the Louvre! The idea that it is beyond human capacity to define in words what the porn merchants can tell at a glance is, well, improbable.

Those whose interests or ideology are advanced by making pornography as widely available as possible like to focus attention on the borderline cases—say, AIDS prevention sites or gynecology sites—suggesting that the mere existence of marginal cases makes any law automatically vague and unenforceable. This is the only area of law, however, where anyone seriously suggests that the existence of marginal cases makes the entire objective unattainable. In defending a manslaughter charge, the borderline difference between "self-defense" and "provocation" can be the difference between jail time and freedom. Should we abandon the law of manslaughter because juries have to make judgment calls?

While a number of different approaches could be taken to defining the reach of an adult domain, it is unreasonable to suggest that it is beyond definition. And the harsh reality is that there is a host of material already on the Internet that is harmful to minors by almost any standard.

"The establishment of [a separate] domain [for online pornography] . . . would do little to reduce access by minors to sexually explicit material on the World Wide Web."

A Separate Domain for Internet Pornography Would Violate Free Speech

Jon Weinberg

Congress established the Child Online Protection Act (COPA) Commission to study ways to protect children from sexually explicit material on the Internet. In the following viewpoint, Jon Weinberg, a law professor at Wayne State University in Detroit, Michigan, testifies that establishing a separate Internet domain such as ".XXX" for pornographic material will have little effect in preventing minors from gaining access to the websites. In addition, he asserts that requiring porn site operators to move their websites to a separate domain would violate the First Amendment.

As you read, consider the following questions:

1. What are the seven generic, three-letter domain names established in 1984, as cited by Weinberg?
2. What is the responsibility of the Internet Corporation for Assigned Names and Numbers?
3. In Weinberg's opinion, why would it be disastrous for the U.S. government to order ICANN to add a separate domain for material harmful to minors?

Excerpted from Jon Weinberg's testimony before the Child Online Protection Act Commission, Washington, D.C., June 8, 2000.

I want to start by providing some background on the management of Internet names and addresses. Internet resources are typically identified by *domain names* such as www.copacommission.org. The domain name space is divided into top-level domains, or TLDs; each TLD is divided into second-level domains, or SLDs; and so on. Under a plan developed in 1984, there are seven "generic," three-letter top-level domains: .com, .net, .org, .edu, .gov (reserved for U.S. government sites), .mil (reserved for U.S. military sites), and .int (reserved for intergovernmental organizations). In addition, there are a whole lot of two-letter "country code" top-level domains, such as .jp, .us and .fr.

When a user, looking for a particular Internet resource, types in a domain name, his computer looks to a set of local *domain name servers* that are specified within its software to find the Internet address corresponding to that domain name. Those local servers, if they don't know the answer, will kick the problem up to a higher level. At the top of the pyramid are a set of *root servers*. Whether a top-level domain is visible in the name space is determined by whether the root servers contain an entry corresponding to that domain. If a user types in a domain name incorporating a top-level domain that the root servers he consults don't recognize, then his computer will be unable to find any resource corresponding to that domain name.

Since 1992, the job of administering the root server, from which all of the other root servers take their lead, has been undertaken by Network Solutions, Inc., a private company, under cooperative agreements with the National Science Foundation and the Commerce Department. Since well before NSI entered the scene, overall policy oversight of the domain name system was in the hands of Dr. Jon Postel at the University of Southern California, under a contract with the Defense Department. NSI followed the directions of Dr. Postel in maintaining, and making changes to, the root servers.

A New System Was Needed

This system, however, wasn't stable. For one thing, as the Internet became increasingly international, it was incongruous for its management to be funded by U.S. government agencies charged with overseeing scientific research projects. Other countries saw the Internet as a global resource, not subject to the narrow whims of the U.S. government, and demanded a voice in its governance. For another thing, the existing domain-name management functions had no robust management structure and no formal accountability to the Internet community.

Finally, the domain-name system was facing policy choices that were beyond the ability of the old system to resolve. Some people wanted to add many new top-level domains to the root zone; others opposed this. Some wanted the domain-name registration process to incorporate strong protection for trademark owners against the registration of names similar to their trademarks; others urged that these disputes should be left to the courts. Many people urged that other firms should be able to compete with Network Solutions in the business of registering domain names, but there was considerable argument over how this should be done. Different people suggested the creation of different new entities to help resolve these issues. These issues were thrashed out, for a period of several years, in what was sometimes called the "DNS wars."

The Development of ICANN

The United States government took a step towards resolving these issues by midwifing the birth of a new, private, nonprofit corporation, with an internationally representative board, called ICANN—the Internet Corporation for Assigned Names and Numbers. The government announced that it would work with ICANN to transfer policy authority over the domain-name system, and specifically charged ICANN with developing policy for the addition of new top-level domains. Initially, the U.S. government proposed that even before ICANN was formed, the government should require the addition of five new top-level domains. In its final policy-statement, called the White Paper, though, the government reversed that position. It concluded that it was better for ICANN to make these decisions itself, based on global input. The White Paper noted that "the challenge of deciding policy for the addition of new domains will be formidable." It expressed support for new domains, but cautioned that "in the short run, a prudent concern for the stability of the system suggests that expansion of [top-level domains] proceed at a deliberate and controlled pace to allow for evolution of the impact of the new [top-level domains] and well-reasoned evolution of the domain space."

ICANN has since engaged in extensive deliberation relating to the possible creation of new top-level domains. In April 2000, the body responsible, within ICANN, for originating policy recommendations on domain-name issues recommended to the ICANN Board that a limited number of new top-level domains be created, in the short term, in a measured and responsible manner. It referred to the possibility of introducing "fully open top-level domains, restricted and chartered top-level domains with limited scope, non-commercial domains and personal domains." It cautioned, however, that there must be "a responsible process for introducing new g[generic]TLDs, which includes ensuring that there is close coordination with organizations dealing with Internet protocols and standards."

It's not at all clear that this whole process will go smoothly. ICANN is still feeling its way, and not all players in the Internet arena fully accept its authority. The U.S. government, indeed, hasn't yet relinquished its own policy authority over the root.

Feasibility

In one sense, it would be "feasible" for Congress to order, tomorrow, the addition of a top-level domain specifically intended for material harmful to minors. Both Network Solutions and ICANN are subject to U.S. jurisdiction. Congress could order Network Solutions to add the new domain to the root servers, and to host the new domain's registry; or it could order ICANN to find a registry to host the new domain, and to request NSI to make the appropriate root server modification. Congress has the raw power to do that.

From the standpoint of the transition of domain-name policymaking authority to ICANN, though, such a move would be disastrous. ICANN is still finding its credibility as a body, independent of national governments, to govern Internet identifiers on behalf of the Internet community. For

Congress to short-circuit ICANN's processes, ordering a particular top-level domain deployed without regard to ICANN's own choices, would strip the ICANN process of its integrity and would make it much harder for anyone to take ICANN seriously as an independent entity for Internet technical management.

Questions About Adult Domains

- We have no objection to the creation of an adult TLD [top-level domain], however it is clear that doing so internationally raises more issues than if it were done only for the U.S. . . .

- Who would define who may register and who may not? Who resolves disputes over compliance? Who should be the gatekeeper for such a TLD? . . .

- If a registrant whose site posted adult material failed to locate that site in an adult TLD, could they then be prosecuted for failing to give adequate notice of the adult nature of their site?

Roger J. Cochetti, "Summary of Remarks on Internet Top Level Domains to the COPA Commission," June 8, 2000.

Further, this would not be the end of government involvement in ICANN decision-making. Other governments would feel entitled to have their own preferences reflected in the domain name space. Other governments would come to ICANN and insist that there be top-level domains created to reflect their own policy preferences. Given the range of speech favored and disfavored by various world governments—including speech promoting Nazism or hate, speech tarnishing the Muslim religion, and so on—it is easy to imagine multiple calls by a wide range of governments for special top-level domains for speech they want to see ghettoized. Indeed, some governments would likely go farther and ask that ICANN use its own bureaucratic apparatus to enforce rules governing who could and could not register in a given domain.

This would damage the U.S. government's effort to transfer domain-name management to a representative, bottom-up, private organization that could expand the name space while imposing minimalist rules. It could contribute to ICANN's failure—and if ICANN fails, one likely result is a splintering of control, with the emergence of new sets of root servers not subject to U.S. authority at all. Alternatively, it could place irresistible pressures on ICANN to become a vehicle for the policy preferences of other world governments, each of them hostile to a different category of speech.

The bottom line is that if the U.S. government were to seek the creation of such a top-level domain as part of the global name space, it would be necessary to work within the ICANN process; it would be destructive to seek to impose that directive from without. Working within the ICANN process, I'll warn you, is difficult, slow and contentious. Further, it's not at all clear how ICANN would appropriately structure such a domain as part of a global name space. . . . Since I am a scholar of filtering and constitutional law I do want to discuss some of the consequences of having this sort of top-level domain at all.

Consequences

To the extent that particular web sites are located only in a particular top-level domain, the enterprise of filtering those sites would be trivial. We would see extensive new filtering, I believe, on routers and servers. That is, if there were a .XXX domain, I expect that a substantial number of Internet service providers would choose to make resources in that domain completely unavailable to their users. Indeed, a significant number of countries would do the same. This would be sufficiently effective, in limiting the commercial reach of sites located in such a domain, that I would expect relatively few U.S.-based sites would voluntarily move there, discontinuing their presence in .com. (On the other hand, some might well move there while maintaining an identical presence in .com.) No sites based outside the U.S. would discontinue their existing sites. The upshot is that the establishment of such a domain, without more, would do little to reduce access by minors to sexually explicit material on the World Wide Web. Any value it had in facilitating filtering would likely be outweighed by its disadvantages in providing to some minors a sure-fire way of finding sexually explicit materials.

The regulatory alternative would be to make use of the

domain mandatory—that is, to make it illegal for U.S.-based speakers to distribute certain categories of speech via the World Wide Web, except at a web site located in the particular top-level domain. This would raise substantial first amendment issues, though. As I mentioned a moment ago, a site located in such a domain would have vastly smaller reach—a substantial number of ISPs would not make it available at all. While individual users would not have to subscribe to those ISPs, a user might well find that if he wanted access to a particular site, he would have to change ISPs in order to do so. Further, any site located in that domain would immediately be branded, in the public eye, as pornography. As a result, requiring a particular speaker to locate in the "harmful to minors" top-level domain would substantially interfere with his ability to get his message out.

First Amendment Issues

This would, in turn, raise all of the First Amendment issues that arose in the *Reno v. ACLU* and COPA [Child Online Protection Act] litigations. How should the class of speakers to be exiled to this domain be defined? [In *Reno v. ACLU*, the Supreme Court ruled the Communications Decency Act of 1995—which tried to regulate the Internet—was unconstitutional. COPA is a second attempt to regulate Internet material that is harmful to minors.]

Recall the Supreme Court's question in *Reno v. ACLU*: "Could a speaker confidently assume that a serious discussion about birth control practices, homosexuality, the First Amendment issues raised by the Appendix to our *Pacifica* opinion, or the consequences of prison rape would not" be covered by the statute? Speakers would have reason to fear, the Court continued, that a prosecutor would read the statute to extend to discussions about safe sexual practices or artistic images including nude subjects. It seems to me plain that it would be unconstitutional to require speakers like those to exile themselves, on pain of criminal prosecution, to a top-level domain from which they could not realistically be heard. That means, though, that such a statute would face the same sort of constitutional obstacles as have prior statutes in this area.

In sum: It would be untenable for the United States government simply to order the creation of a new top-level domain for material harmful to minors. Rather, if it wishes to see such a domain created, it will have to work within the ICANN policy process. The benefits of having such a domain, though, are clouded at best. If use of the domain is not made mandatory, its mere existence will do little to reduce access by minors to sexually explicit material on the World Wide Web. But any statute purporting to make use of the domain mandatory would raise serious constitutional problems.

Periodical Bibliography

The following articles have been selected to supplement the diverse views presented in this chapter. Addresses are provided for periodicals not indexed in the *Readers' Guide to Periodical Literature*, the *Alternative Press Index*, the *Social Sciences Index*, or the *Index to Legal Periodicals and Books*.

Amy Adler	"Photography on Trial," *Index on Censorship*, May/June 1996.
Walter Berns	"Pornography Versus Democracy," *Society*, September/October 1999.
Francis Canavan	"Speech That Matters," *Society*, September/October 1999.
Philip Elmer Dewitt	"On a Screen Near You: Cyberporn," *Time*, July 3, 1995.
Bruce Handy	"Beyond the Pale," *Time*, March 16, 1998.
Malcolm Jones	"Can Art Photography Be Kiddie Porn?" *Newsweek*, March 9, 1998.
Wendy Kaminer	"The Chador Hits Cyberspace," *Nation*, March 9, 1999.
Irving Kristol	"Liberal Censorship and the Common Culture," *Society*, September/October 1999.
Norman Podhoretz	"'Lolita,' My Mother-in-Law, the Marquis de Sade, and Larry Flynt," *Commentary*, April 1997.
Joshua Quittner	"Unshackling Net Speech," *Time*, July 7, 1997.
Jeffrey Rosen	"Zoned Out," *New Republic*, March 31, 1997.
Frances Smith	"Protecting Kids on the Internet," *Consumers' Research Magazine*, January 1999.
Laurence H. Tribe	"The Internet vs. the First Amendment," *The New York Times*, April 28, 1999.
Julia Wilkins	"Protecting Our Children from Internet Smut: Moral Duty or Moral Panic?" *Humanist*, September/October 1997.
Melana Zyla	"Controlling Cyberporn Soon May Be a Reality," *USA Today*, April 8, 1998.

CHAPTER 3

Should Schools and Libraries Practice Censorship?

Chapter Preface

The federal government is making a concerted effort to ensure that all public schools have computer access to the Internet. It is providing funds for computers, low-cost connection rates, and other incentives to see that schools get online. But many teachers and parents are concerned about children going online in schools and libraries because of the proliferation and accessibility of X-rated websites. According to a 2000 report released by the Family Research Council, "pornography is becoming a staple in one library after another because adults and children are accessing it through unfiltered library computer terminals."

To protect their students from inadvertently encountering sexually explicit material on the Internet, many schools and libraries are installing software filters on their computers that block access to prohibited sites. Advocates of software filters support government efforts to require the use of filters in schools and public libraries. They contend that obscene speech such as online pornography is not entitled to First Amendment protection. In addition, they argue, if the library does not carry hard copies of pornographic magazines such as *Playboy* or *Hustler*, why should the library make them available online?

Opponents of filters maintain, however, that the filters are a violation of the right to free speech. Brock Meeks and Declan McCullagh, authors of an online exposé on filters, contend that software filters are designed to do more than merely block access to pornographic sites. "The smut-censors say they're going after porn, but they quietly restrict political speech," Meeks and McCullagh contend. Barbara Miner, editor of *Rethinking Schools*, agrees, arguing that software filters "routinely block access to thousands of World Wide Web pages, chat rooms, newsgroups and other Internet options" on such topics as the Holocaust, Islam, AIDS/HIV, gay rights, and feminism.

The use of software filters is just one of the issues considered in the following chapter on censorship in schools and libraries. This topic is especially controversial because of the view that children's attitudes and beliefs are influenced by their education and learning environment.

*"Reasonable limits to intellectual freedom
for the good of the community should
frighten no one."*

Libraries Should Restrict Access to Offensive Books

Helen Chaffee Biehle

In the following viewpoint, Helen Chaffee Biehle contends that libraries have abandoned their role of acting *in loco parentis* (in place of the parent) in protecting young children from inappropriate material. Libraries now permit children to view and check out obscene material that they would not be permitted to see or buy outside of libraries. Biehle, who is a teacher in Ohio, argues that libraries should once again act as censors and keep inappropriate material out of the hands of children.

As you read, consider the following questions:
1. What are a library's three arguments for why it cannot censor material for children, as cited by Biehle?
2. According to the author, how does the American Library Association characterize librarians who accept and make moral judgments about offensive materials?
3. What does Article 5 of the ALA's Library Bill of Rights advocate, as cited by Biehle?

Excerpted from "The Internet and the Seduction of the American Public Library," by Helen Chaffee Biehle, on the Family Friendly Libraries website, found at www.fflibraries.org/Basic_Docs/biehle.htm (downloaded 11/7/00).

"We could drop your kids off at the library while you and I finish our shopping," I said to my young friend. She looked shocked. "I never let my kids go to the library alone!"

I did a double-take. I was, after all, a library lover. As a teacher for 25 years, I had gone to the library more often than I'd gone to the grocer. But I had not looked into the youth division since my grown children had used it.

My friend sputtered on. "The librarians say they have special rights, so they can't protect children any more and can't notify parents. And parents don't have any rights. If we complain they call us 'censors.' I dare you to go into the youth section over at County Library and see what's there. Some of the stuff will curl your hair."

A Purveyor of Obscenity

The next morning, I opened the local paper and understood instantly what my friend was getting at. There in bold print was the story of Mrs. Cindy Friedman, her 12-year-old son and the county library. She had refused her son permission to buy 2 Live Crew's rap tape, *As Nasty As They Wanna Be*, as had the local record store on the legal grounds that he was underage. I remembered that this was the very tape that had been judged by a federal judge to be obscene and whose seller had been arrested, and whose performers had been arrested for an obscene performance in Florida. True to its title, the tape is nasty, indeed, glorifying rape, with men's voices shouting "I'm gonna break you" and "I wanna see you bleed!" over the plaintive voice of a young girl crying "No! No!" All of the lyrics on the tape are unremitting gutter profanity, and all are about violent and casual sex which gleefully celebrates sadistic cruelty toward women. Imagine Mrs. Friedman's astonishment when she discovered that her son, on an innocent trip to the library, had not only found the offending tape in the library's collection, but had been allowed to check it out with his library card with no questions asked.

According to the Cleveland *Sun Messenger* account, Mrs. Friedman, with the perfectly normal reactions of a responsible parent, fell into the library's ideological trap. "If he has to be 18 to buy the tape, he should have to be 18 to take it out of the library," she said. (Zap!) "The Library Bill of Rights forbids discrimination on the basis of age," said the library head.

"The library should have a system of warning parents what kids are taking out," said Mrs. Friedman. (Zap!) "That would be CENSORSHIP. Besides, librarians cannot act *in loco parentis.*" (Excuse me. Who said so? They had formerly been doing this, just as teachers had, for many, many years.) What was going on here? Was there to be no apology to Mrs. Friedman for what columnist John Leo calls the cultural equivalent of poison gas? I reached for the telephone. "I'd like to speak to the director of the Cuyahoga [Ohio] County Library system." (This is a system with 28 libraries and 440,000 patrons.) When the director answered, I questioned her current policy on children, and asked for some adult supervision in the purchasing department. She was completely calm and utterly un-apologetic. Much later, I learned that her calm came from following the detailed instructions given by the library's *Intellectual Freedom Manual* for handling irate taxpayers like me.

The Library's Defense

The Library Director's first defense was diversity. "Neither you nor I might approve of *As Nasty As They Wanna Be*, she said, but we serve a very diverse population." I assumed that this was a code word for minority groups. But, not long afterward, my trust in her excuse about diversity began to evaporate as I read news accounts about the African-American parents demonstration against Rap recordings and their effect on their kids. And later, the whole country began seeing news reports about Rap performers who had been arrested and charged with rape or murder.

The library head's second line of defense was philosophic. "Not to buy the tape would be making a moral judgment," she said. "We can't do that." (Not make a moral judgment? Can we not judge that cruelty is wrong? Can we not agree that cruelty packaged as entertainment and given to children is morally indefensible?) I couldn't resist recommending a book to the library head: British philosopher Mary Midgley's *Can't We Make Moral Judgements* (sic). (That was in 1991.

Who would have guessed that five years later a commercial retailer, WalMart, would put libraries to shame by making moral judgments? It would refuse to sell recordings with obscene lyrics and album covers. The record companies would respond by offering cleaned-up performance versions. Bottom line: Parents could trust Wal-Mart.)

The library head's third defense was the Library Bill of Rights, "You need to read this," she said. "It states clearly that we can't keep materials from children on the basis of age. You can find a copy of it in the American Library Association's *Intellectual Freedom Manual*." I hung up the receiver and drove like a demon to the nearest library. I was determined to find out what had caused this doleful change in a formerly beloved institution. Sure enough, buried in the chapters of that ALA paperback manual is the entire history of who changed our libraries, how and when.

A Rejected Responsibility

The library with which most Americans over the age of thirty grew up was the creation of people like William Fletcher and Arthur Bostwick, who, writing at the turn of the century, encouraged librarians to accept responsibility for the library's moral influence in the community. And this is the heart of the change: today the ALA resoundingly rejects this responsibility as naive and old-fashioned. Its official statements ridicule and ostracize librarians who do not comply with this rejection and library schools teach the new doctrine. The acceptance of moral responsibility for children in the library is now called "unprofessional"; making a responsible moral judgment about materials purchased for the library is called "elitist," and the librarian who is brave enough to do either is labeled a "censor.". . .

Libraries, before the 1960's, had great local autonomy. Librarians were free to make moral judgments and were thus free to acquire the best available materials for their library collections. There were separate collections for children and adults, and, until the 1960's, the American library shared common values with its public. . . .

The moral tone of today's public library is a casualty of the culture wars which began in the 1960's. During the social turmoil of that period, Judith Krug, a Phi Beta Kappa graduate of the University of Pittsburgh and the Library School of the University of Chicago, was in 1967, appointed director of the ALA's new Office of Intellectual Freedom, a position which she still holds today. A true child of the Sixties, Ms. Krug appears to have rejected the library's trusted role as the repository of civilization, seeing it instead as an engine of social change. She has worked tirelessly to make it so, forging, for example, strong links with the American Civil Liberties Union, on whose board she served for three years while carrying on her job as head of the OIF. She has been very successful in promulgating the ACLU's views within the country's libraries, and the ACLU has honored her with awards.

The policies of the ACLU are based on a philosophical nihilism which sees the freedom of the autonomous self as the highest good, and all censorship as evil. This has not changed since its founding by Roger Baldwin at the turn of the century. According to George Grant's 1989 study, the ACLU believes that children should have the same rights as adults, that pornography should be protected by the Constitution, and that the tiniest limitation of any expression will lead automatically to totalitarian repression. The current president, Nadine Strossen, is the author of *Defending Pornography: Free Speech, Sex and the Fight for Women's Rights.*

Judith Krug is also director of the Freedom to Read Foundation, which she herself describes as an activist group. Like the ACLU, its attorneys stand ready to sue in library censorship cases. . . .

Age and Libraries

It is apparently from these groups that the ALA has absorbed the philosophy that children do not need protection from socially destructive materials. Consistent with this view, in 1967, Ms. Krug's right-hand man, Ervin Gaines, suggested in a national ALA meeting that the word "age" be added to the Library Bill of Rights, so that any child of any age could access adult material in libraries. By 1972, the ALA council had approved Article 5, "A person's right to use a library should not be denied or abridged because of origin, age, background or views."

This one word has led to hundreds of conflicts between communities (especially parents) and their libraries. But instead of deleting the word "age" from Article 5, the ALA has developed strategies for doing battle with the public.

Easy Access to Forbidden Books

School librarians have been getting bolder with the materials they order for school libraries which, unlike the general public libraries, have little or no opportunity for parental oversight. Only when books are brought home are the parents aware of their child's reading choices. Works promoting the occult (including one book directing a step-by-step deal with the devil), gay rights, sexual freedom and "reproductive choice," plus teen magazines displaying an increasing number of sexually explicit articles, have raised the ire of parents when they appear so accessibly on school shelves away from family supervision.

Even elementary school libraries have raised hackles by supplying students with a collection of "Goosebumps," "Fear Street" and other cult kiddie books often forbidden on the home front. Though some teachers admit that genre is of low educational quality, they claim such materials prod reluctant readers to read. But studies show such students mostly only progress to more books within the same genre, not on to better literature. Some of the more sensitive school librarians, in defiance of the American Library Association creed (the only good access is everything for everybody, regardless of content and age), lay aside some of the more explicit or controversial materials and keep them on a shelf they alone monitor for occasional access for older students or visiting parents.

Karen Jo Gounaud, "Battle of the Bawdy Books," February 7, 1998.

The first strategy was to "interpret" Article 5 for libraries and to pressure them into obeying the will of ALA headquarters. During the anti-draft riots of the 1960's, Congress had lowered the voting age to 18. College students had pressed for more personal and sexual rights, denying that colleges any longer had the right to act *in loco parentis* (in place of the parent). The ALA then moved to deny that librarians, who had been acting *in loco parentis* for children in the library for not quite 100 years, any longer had that right.

In the case of the colleges, students were rejecting established authority. But in the library's case, we are confronted with the strange spectacle of established authority rejecting its own responsibility to children and their parents.

Article 5 of the Library Bill of Rights does not actually mention *in loco parentis*, but the Intellectual Freedom Manual lays down the new rules. Many libraries, used to a tradition of local control, continued separate card files for children and continued to act as authority figures responsible to the community. In response, the Office of Intellectual Freedom drafted an "Interpretation of Free Access to Minors" and sent it to librarians all across the country. (It was this statement that cut off the partnership between parents and librarians and caused what parents see as a betrayal of their trust.)

The Statement labels as "unprofessional," any librarians who continue to notify or act for the parents. Librarians who do not follow the ALA line are accused of being "in violation of Article 5 of the Library Bill of Rights." I asked Ms. Krug if librarians were legally bound to follow the Statement of Interpretation. "No," she said. "It's a philosophical statement. But 55,000 librarians adhere to it.". . .

Libraries Should Censor

It is a fact that most of the material about which parents complain would never have been found in the library before the 1970's. And, had the Internet been in existence, the ALA would have found the idea of access to pornography in the library to be simply out of the question. The enormous change in attitudes toward the selection of materials for the library is vividly illustrated in the ALA's own literature. For example, Arthur Bostwick, President of ALA in 1908, said in his inauguration speech:

> Books that distinctly commend what is wrong, that teach how to sin and how pleasant sin is . . . are increasingly popular, tempting . . . the publishers to produce, the bookseller to exploit. . . . Thank heaven they do not tempt the librarian.

In his 1929 book, *The American Public Library*, he says "Nobody can buy every title that is published, and we should discriminate by picking out what is best."

In 1956 the Division of Public Libraries of the ALA Coordinating Committee published guidelines for materials selection which were taught by library schools. At first glance, the following guideline looks like a statement by today's ALA:

> The collection must contain various opinions which apply to . . . controversial questions . . . including unpopular and unorthodox positions. . . . Selection must resist efforts of groups to deny access to materials in the name of political, moral or religious beliefs.

But then, we remember the context. Library collections were still separate for children and adults. The Supreme Court had not yet let down the bars against indecent material. Libraries still had great freedom from the heavy hand of the ALA. In that context, the statement fits comfortably with the Committee's other important guidelines for materials selection:

> The library continually seeks the best. . . . Materials acquired should meet high standards of quality in content, expression and format. . . . Factual accuracy . . . significance of subject, sincerity and responsibility of opinion must be considered.

(Madonna or 2 Live Crew in the library? Not under these guidelines!) Now fast-forward to 1996 and Mr. Conable, speaking for the ALA in the *Intellectual Freedom Manual.* He says librarians should not "narrowly limit collection scope on the basis of purely subjective factors such as 'quality' or 'popularity,' which require outside endorsement in the form of reviews or recommended lists . . . or which are written in a way to justify the exclusion of controversial material. . . ." *"If material remains unordered, un-catalogued or un-circulated, . . . censorship has occurred"* (Emphasis added.) Here, the use of any kind of responsible judgment is equated with censorship, thus making it impossible for a librarian to build excellence into a collection. . . .

Tax-supported libraries allow children access today to material so destructive that before the Internet, Ted Bundy could only get it from adult bookstores off-limits to children. In libraries, ironically, nothing is off-limits to children. Yet libraries are currently immune to obscenity and "harm to minors" laws. The seriousness of this situation is brought home by the fact that were a librarian to provide some of the material in question to a child on the street *outside* the library, that adult could be subject to arrest. . . .

Mild Limits on Freedom

Everyone accepts, for the good of the community, mild limits on freedom in other areas: we must have a license to drive; we stop at red lights; we do not even fish without a license. Reasonable limits to intellectual freedom for the good of the community should frighten no one, for these limits were once observed in this country with a correspondingly better quality of life, including the safety of children.

Our quarrel with ALA is over their belief in philosopher Jean-Paul Sartre's absolute freedom of the individual. This kind of freedom rejects responsibility and is blind to consequences. On the other hand, those who reject the ALA philosophy believe in the "freedom to do as one ought." This classic definition of freedom involves responsibility and weighs consequences to the community, especially its children. Only this kind of freedom is appropriate in a truly civilized society.

*"If government officials sought to remove or
restrict access to a book on the ground that
government officials opposed an idea in
that book, the removal of the book clearly
would violate the First Amendment."*

American Library Association Intellectual Freedom Policies and the First Amendment

Bruce J. Ennis

Bruce J. Ennis is the general counsel to the Freedom to Read
Foundation, an organization that promotes and protects
freedom of speech. In the following viewpoint, Ennis argues
that the policies established by the American Library Asso
ciation allowing minors unrestricted access to library materials are consistent with the U.S. Constitution. Public and
school libraries cannot remove or restrict a minor's access to
books or other materials without violating the First Amendment, he maintains. Banning or restricting access to a book
because of the ideas it contains is censorship, he contends,
and therefore illegal.

As you read, consider the following questions:

1. According to Ennis, when may access to library materials
   be legally restricted?
2. What was the Supreme Court's decision in *Board of
   Education v. Pico*, as cited by the author?
3. What are the only circumstances under which books may
   be removed from libraries, according to a ruling of a
   California appellate court?

[F]rom time to time, the Foundation receives questions regarding the relationship of the ALA intellectual freedom policies to the First Amendment. People often want to know whether or not ALA's policies go beyond the First Amendment. Since the question is key to Foundation activities, we asked our counsel to comment. *His response follows:*] You requested our input on the following two questions: (1) whether the American Library Association (ALA) goes beyond judicially mandated First Amendment protections in its policies; and (2) if it is not a violation of First Amendment rights to control access to some materials because of a theft or vandalism problem, whether it would be a constitutional violation to control access to material because it may be inappropriate for children below a certain age. We address each issue separately.

First, the policies of the ALA are based on, and consistent with, federal and state constitutional protections as interpreted by the judiciary. Thus, ALA policies safeguard the rights of free speech of all patrons to the extent protected by either the federal or state constitution. It is manifest that the ALA policies safeguard all speech protected by the First Amendment of the United States Constitution. Additionally, ALA policies protect all speech secured by a state constitution even if those protections are broader than those encompassed in the federal constitution. For example, the First Amendment of the federal constitution has been interpreted as providing more limited protection for commercial as opposed to political speech. If a state constitution were interpreted as providing greater protection for commercial speech in a particular jurisdiction, that speech would be encompassed in the ALA policies. A state might choose not to place any restrictions on speech. (Libraries in each state, however, should check with their state statutes to see whether or what kind of obscenity or harmful to minors laws exist, and they should ask their attorneys whether such laws apply to the library.) ALA policies would, therefore, direct that all expressive materials in that particular state were constitutionally protected and encompassed within the ALA policies. In the spirit of providing the greatest access to information and ideas, ALA policies were intended to encompass the broadest interpretation of protection for free speech.

Second, courts have held that children are entitled to the protections afforded by the First Amendment. Thus, courts have held that governments (including school boards) may not restrict minors' access to materials based on the viewpoint expressed therein. Although it may not violate the First Amendment to restrict access to a special or rare collection because of concerns of theft or vandalism, it would violate the First Amendment to restrict access to expressive materials, or ban them entirely, on the basis of viewpoint—even if the restrictions were directed to minors. The Supreme Court has held that the critical inquiry centers on motivation.

In B*oard of Education v. Pico*, 457 *U.S. 853 (1982)*, the Supreme Court considered whether a school board's removal of books from a school library violated the First Amendment rights of the students. A plurality held:

> [W]hether petitioners' removal of books from their school library denied respondents their First Amendment rights depends upon the motivation behind petitioners' actions. If petitioners *intended* by their removal decision to deny respondents access to ideas with which petitioners disagreed, and if this intent was the decisive factor in petitioners' decision, then petitioners have exercised their discretion in violation of the Constitution.

Id. At 871 (emphasis in text). The plurality opinion emphasized that "local school boards may not remove books from school library shelves simply because they dislike the ideas contained in those books and seek by their removal to 'prescribe what shall be orthodox in politics, nationalism, religion, or other matters of opinion.'" *Id.* At 872 (citation omitted) . . .

Other courts have followed *Pico*'s guidance that *motivation* is the key question in book removal cases. Thus, lower courts have suggested that although school boards have broader discretion in questions of school curriculum—provided the decisions are reasonably related to legitimate pedagogical concerns—removal of books from the *school library* implicates protected First Amendment rights. It follows that government would have even less justification to remove books or restrict access to books in the *public library* on the ground that such books are not suitable for children.

Public libraries wisely leave the decision of reading mate-

Restrictions Must Be Limited

It is certainly valid for any group of people to organize and approach their locally controlled library with issues of concern. Yet there are limits to the restriction of the rights of others, even if those others are your children. The belief that it should be possible to prevent a child from reading science, medical information, or competing religious views is patently absurd. If a parent wishes to thus restrict a child, handcuffing him or her to a bedpost will do as nicely.

Robert Riehemann, *Free Inquiry*, Spring 1997.

rial to the patrons—or their parents. Unless there is an applicable Harmful to Minors Act, a policy of free access (limited only by parental decisions of appropriateness for very young children) provides the greatest insulation for the library from constitutional attack for restricting access to materials protected by the First Amendment. Restrictions on access that are not based on valid administrative reasons (such as reasonable concerns about theft and vandalism) could be interpreted as restrictions based on disagreement by the government with the views expressed in the material. Thus, if government officials sought to remove or restrict access to a book on the ground that government officials opposed an idea in that book, the removal of the book clearly would violate the First Amendment.

Third, it is possible that enabling statutes governing libraries could be useful. Checking those statutes will help determine whether they define the role of the library in removing materials. For example, in *Wexner v. Anderson, 209 Cal. App. 3d 1438, 258 Cal. Rptr. 26 (Cal. App. 3d Dist. 1989)*, a California appellate court held that a school district could not forbid high school students from reading books in a school library collection on the ground that materials were not "socially acceptable." The California appellate court did not reach the constitutional issue. Instead, the appellate court held that the statutory authority provided to libraries did not permit removal of books from the school library (or presumably any public library in California) based on their content or "social acceptability." 258 Cal. Rptr. at 36. The court held that books could only be removed if they were "not fit for service" (interpreted by the court as "worn out") or "no longer needed by the course of study" (interpreted by the court to apply only to textbooks). The courts thus concluded that "*a county librarian* or superintendent of schools running a library has no authority, even with the approval of the board, to remove a book because of objectionable conduct." *Id.* (emphasis added)

"The common sense answer . . . is to restrict children under 18 to certain, filtered computers in a protected area of the library."

Libraries Should Use Software Filters for the Internet

Kathleen Parker

Kathleen Parker argues in the following viewpoint that pornography on the Internet is easily accessible. Parker, a syndicated columnist, believes libraries should cooperate with parents to keep young children from being exposed to online pornography. One such option is to employ filtering software that will block access to X-rated sites.

As you read, consider the following questions:
1. What percentage of libraries responded to a study by the Family Research Council on the Internet pornography on library computers, as cited by the author?
2. How many incidents were reported by libraries of patrons accessing pornographic sites on public library computers, according to Parker?
3. What solution does Parker recommend for students researching a topic that is blocked by a library computer?

Ted's jaw dropped perceptibly as I described how easily he could find pornography on the Internet. It's as simple as pushing a button, I said.

No, it couldn't be *that* easy, he said.

It's that easy.

Ted is brand new to the Internet. He just bought his first computer and can't wait to get on-line. He's also the father of a 7-year-old daughter who probably knows more about computers—and pornography—than her ancient 35-year-old dad.

If she's been to some of our nation's public libraries, she might have seen plenty. After all, children on their way to pull *Goodnight Moon* off the shelf can glimpse everything from bestiality to torture just by walking past a terminal where porn is being viewed. And there's no limit to the deviance young Internet surfers can encounter on a public computer.

Hel-lo Ted and all you other clueless parents out there: nap's over. The Internet is happening; pornography is ubiquitous; no one is watching your children.

Dangerous Access

A new study released by the Family Research Council, "Dangerous Access, 2000 Edition: Uncovering Internet Pornography in America's Libraries," says that the American Library Association (ALA) is ignoring a "sea of evidence" that "Internet pornography and related sex crimes are a serious problem in America's libraries."

The study used the Freedom of Information Act to get library reports of Internet traffic. With only 29 percent of libraries responding, researchers found 2,000 incidents of patrons, many of them children, accessing pornography in America's public libraries.

Considering the number of people using libraries, 2,000 doesn't seem like a "sea," or even a large lake, unless your child happens to be one of those swimming in the slime. But even 10 million "hits" wouldn't likely change the ALA's position against mandated filtering. The onus, says the ALA, is on parents. Besides, they add, filters are ineffective in that they block legitimate research as well as pornography.

The ALA's favorite example is breast cancer. A typical filtering system would block access to any site containing the word "breast," thus thwarting important information about breast cancer or, say, breast-feeding.

Library Incidents Involving Internet Pornography

In the summer of 1999, the Family Research Council sent out more than 14,000 requests to the nation's 9,767 library systems seeking information about incidents involving pornography on the libraries' computers. The number of libraries that responded to the freedom-of-information requests was 452. Their responses were tabulated and classified as noted below:

Incident Reports, Patron Complaints, and News Stories	Number
Child Accessing Pornography	472
Adult Accessing Pornography	962
Adult Exposing Children to Pornography	106
Adult Accessing Inappropriate Material	225
Attempted Molestation	5
Child Porn Being Accessed	41
Child Accidentally Viewing Pornography	26
Adult Accidentally Viewing Pornography	23
Child Accessing Inappropriate Material	41
Harassing Staff with Pornography	25
Pornography Left for Children	23
Pornography Left on Printer or Screen	113
Total Number of Incidents	2,062

David Burt, *Dangerous Access, 2000 Edition: Uncovering Internet Pornography in America's Libraries*, 2000.

More important, the ALA argues that blocking pornography constitutes censorship and interferes with intellectual freedom. They make their case on the ALA Web site (www.ala.org), citing historical incidents of people being "burned at the stake, forced to drink poison, crucified, ostracized and vilified" for what they wrote and believed.

I'm no fan of burning people at the stake, except on the

occasional Tuesday, but a little vilification would be welcome. It's ironic that parents who have bothered to distract their children from television to cultivate an interest in books ultimately have less to worry about from the tube than they do from the public library.

The ALA's attitude, meanwhile, is tough luck. As explained on their Web site: "Parents who believe that the current state of society and communications make it difficult to shield their children must nevertheless find a way to cope with what they see as that reality within the context of their own family."

Reasonable Compromises

Parents trying to cope have pushed for reasonable compromises, such as segregating filtered and unfiltered computers.

Some libraries have been more cooperative than others. Almost all have policies about Internet use, whether requiring a parental signature for children's use or limiting on-line time. But until we find the guts and sense to define obscenity, none are sufficient protection absent a parent or adult to monitor children on the Internet.

The common sense answer, meantime, is to restrict children under 18 to certain, filtered computers in a protected area of the library. If the kid is researching breast cancer for a school project and can't find the link, well, guess what. Librarians are there to help. Aren't they?

*"Parents—and only parents—have the right
and responsibility to restrict their own
children's access—and only their own
children's access—to library resources,
including the Internet."*

Statement on Internet Filtering

Intellectual Freedom Committee,
American Library Association

The Intellectual Freedom Committee of the American Library Association (the oldest and largest national library organization in the world) works to educate librarians and the public on the importance of providing individuals with free access to all points of view. In the following viewpoint, the committee contends that software filters, which are designed to block offensive or pornographic sites on the Internet, are unconstitutional because they discriminate against speech that is protected by the First Amendment. It is the responsibility of parents—not libraries—to restrict children's access to inappropriate materials, the committee maintains.

As you read, consider the following questions:
1. What was the U.S. Supreme Court's fundamental holding in its decision released June 26, 1997, according to the ALA?
2. What examples does the ALA give of how blocking or filtering software restricts access to the Internet?
3. Why are software filters antithetical to the mission of libraries, according to the ALA?

On June 26, 1997, the United States Supreme Court issued a sweeping reaffirmation of core First Amendment principles and held that communications over the Internet deserve the highest level of Constitutional protection.

The Court's most fundamental holding was that communications on the Internet deserve the same level of Constitutional protection as books, magazines, newspapers, and speakers on a street corner soapbox. The Court found that the Internet "constitutes a vast platform from which to address and hear from a world-wide audience of millions of readers, viewers, researchers, and buyers," and that "any person with a phone line can become a town crier with a voice that resonates farther than it could from any soapbox."

For libraries, the most critical holding of the Supreme Court is that libraries that make content available on the Internet can continue to do so with the same Constitutional protections that apply to the books on libraries' shelves. The Court's conclusion that "the vast democratic fora of the Internet" merit full constitutional protection will also serve to protect libraries that provide their patrons with access to the Internet. The Court recognized the importance of enabling individuals to receive speech from the entire world and to speak to the entire world. Libraries provide those opportunities to many who would not otherwise have them. The Supreme Court's decision protects that access.

The use in libraries of software filters which block constitutionally protected speech is inconsistent with the United States Constitution and federal law and may lead to legal exposure for the library and its governing authorities. The American Library Association affirms that the use of filtering software by libraries to block access to constitutionally protected speech violates the Library Bill of Rights.

What Is Blocking/Filtering Software?

Blocking/filtering software is a mechanism used to:
  • restrict access to Internet content, based on an internal database of the product, or;
  • restrict access to Internet content through a database maintained external to the product itself, or;
  • restrict access to Internet content to certain ratings as-

signed to those sites by a third party, or;
- restrict access to Internet content by scanning content, based on a keyword, phrase or text string, or;
- restrict access to Internet content based on the source of the information.

Problems with Filtering Software in Libraries

Publicly supported libraries are governmental institutions subject to the First Amendment, which forbids them from restricting information based on viewpoint or content discrimination.

Libraries are places of inclusion rather than exclusion. Current blocking/filtering software prevents not only access to what some may consider "objectionable" material, but also blocks information protected by the First Amendment. The result is that legal and useful material will inevitably be blocked. Examples of sites that have been blocked by popular commercial blocking/filtering products include those on breast cancer, AIDS, women's rights, and animal rights.

Filters can impose the producer's viewpoint on the community.

Producers do not generally reveal what is being blocked, or provide methods for users to reach sites that were inadvertently blocked.

Criteria used to block content are vaguely defined and subjectively applied.

The vast majority of Internet sites are informative and useful. Blocking/filtering software often blocks access to materials it is not designed to block.

Most blocking/filtering software is designed for the home market. Filters are intended to respond to the preferences of parents making decisions for their own children. Libraries are responsible for serving a broad and diverse community with different preferences and views. Blocking Internet sites is antithetical to library missions because it requires the library to limit information access.

In a library setting, filtering today is a one-size-fits-all "solution," which cannot adapt to the varying ages and maturity levels of individual users.

A role of librarians is to advise and assist users in selecting information resources. Parents—and only parents—have the right and responsibility to restrict their own children's access—and only their own children's access—to library resources, including the Internet. Librarians do not serve in loco parentis.

Library use of blocking/filtering software creates an implied contract with parents that their children *will not* be able to access material on the Internet that they do not wish their children to read or view. Libraries will be unable to fulfill this implied contract, due to the technological limitations of the software, thus exposing themselves to possible legal liability and litigation.

Laws prohibiting the production or distribution of child pornography and obscenity apply to the Internet. These laws provide protection for libraries and their users.

"The strongest reason for enacting hate-speech rules on campuses . . . is that they are necessary to promote equality."

Campus Speech Codes Are Necessary

Richard Delgado and Jean Stefancic

Richard Delgado and Jean Stefancic are coauthors of *Must We Defend Nazis? Hate Speech, Pornography, and the New First Amendment*, from which this viewpoint is excerpted. They argue that speech codes regulating hate speech on school campuses are necessary to combat racism and sexual harassment and to prevent the infliction of emotional distress with words. Delgado and Stefancic contend that the right to permit hate speech cannot override an individual's right not to be subjected to hate speech. Furthermore, they assert that to demean people—and to protect such speech and actions—is paternalistic and arrogant.

As you read, consider the following questions:
1. What possible reasons do the authors give for the rise in the number of reported cases of hate speech?
2. According to Delgado and Stefancic, what two provisions must be included in a direct prohibition of hate speech on campus?
3. How do the authors define *hubris*?

Beginning in the 1980s, many campuses began noticing a sharp rise in the number of incidents of hate-ridden speech directed at minorities, gays, lesbians, and others. Experts are divided on the causes of the upsurge. A few argue that the increase is the result of better reporting or heightened sensitivity on the part of the minority community. Most, however, believe that the changes are real, noting that they are consistent with a sharp rise in attacks on foreigners, immigrants, and ethnic minorities occurring in many Western industrialized nations. This general rise, in turn, may be prompted by deteriorating economies and increased competition for jobs. It may reflect an increase in populations of color, due to immigration patterns and high birthrates. It may be related to the ending of the Cold War and competition between the two superpowers.

Whatever its cause, campus racism is of great concern to many educators and university officials. At the University of Wisconsin, for example, the number of black students dropped sharply in the wake of highly publicized incidents of racism. Faced with negative publicity and declining minority enrollments, some campuses established programs aimed at racial awareness. Others broadened their curriculum to include more multicultural offerings, events, and theme houses. Still others enacted hate-speech codes that prohibit slurs and disparaging remarks directed against persons on account of their ethnicity, religion, or sexual orientation. Sometimes these codes are patterned after existing torts or the fighting-words exception to the First Amendment. One at the University of Texas, for example, bars personalized insults that amount to intentional infliction of emotional distress. Another, at the University of California at Berkeley, prohibits "those personally abusive epithets which, when directly addressed to any ordinary person, are . . . likely to provoke a violent reaction whether or not they actually do so."

Court Challenges

It was not long before these codes were challenged in court. In *Doe v. University of Michigan*, the university unsuccessfully defended a student conduct code that prohibited verbal or physical behavior that "stigmatizes or victimizes" any individual on the basis of various immutable and cultural characteristics, and that "[c]reates an intimidating, hostile or demeaning environment." Citing Supreme Court precedent that requires speech regulations to be clear and precise, the district court found Michigan's code fatally vague and overbroad. Two years later, in *UWM Post, Inc. v. Board of Regents*, a different federal court considered a University of Wisconsin rule that prohibited disruptive epithets directed against an individual because of his or her race, religion, or sexual orientation. The court invalidated the rule, finding the measure overly broad and ambiguous. The court refused to apply a balancing test that would weigh the social value of the speech with its harmful effect, and found the rule's similarity to Title VII doctrine insufficient to satisfy constitutional requirements.

Finally, the Supreme Court in *R.A.V. v. City of St. Paul* struck down a city ordinance that selectively prohibited certain forms of racist expression. In *R.A.V.*, a white youth had burned a cross on the lawn of a black family. The local prosecutor charged him with disorderly conduct under an ordinance that forbade expression aimed at "arousing anger, alarm or resentment in others on the basis of race, color, creed, religion or gender." Even after adopting the Minnesota Supreme Court's construction of the ordinance to apply only to fighting words, the Supreme Court found it unconstitutional. Fighting words, although regulable in some circumstances, are not entirely devoid of First Amendment protection; in particular, they may not be prohibited based on the content of the message. Not only did the ordinance discriminate based on content, but it further discriminated based on viewpoint by choosing to punish only those fighting words which expressed an opinion with which the city disagreed.

More recent decisions have been more supportive of the efforts of some authorities to take action against racism. In *Wisconsin v. Mitchell*, a black man was convicted of aggravated battery for severely beating a white youth. Because the defendant selected the victim for his race, the defendant's sentence was increased by an additional two years under a Wisconsin penalty-enhancement statute. The United States Supreme Court affirmed the statute's constitutionality, holding that motive, and more specifically racial hatred, can be considered in determining the sentence of a convicted defendant. The Court explained that while "abstract beliefs, however obnoxious" are protected under the First Amendment, they are not protected once those beliefs express themselves in commission of a crime. . . .

The Feasibility of Regulating Hate Speech

The recent scholarly interest in torts-based approaches provides a final development suggesting the feasibility of regulating hate speech. Several scholars advocate regulating hate speech through the torts of intentional infliction of emotional distress or group defamation. These scholars propose that the law of tort might be tapped to supply models for harm-based codes that would pass constitutional muster. They emphasize that tort law's historic role in redressing personal wrongs, its neutrality, and its relative freedom from constitutional restraints are powerful advantages for rules aimed at curbing hate speech.

At present, then, case law and scholarly commentary suggest that hate-speech restrictions may be drafted in compliance with the First Amendment. Given the feasibility of enacting hate-speech codes, coupled with the continued rise of racism on college campuses, the future seems to lie squarely in the hands of policymakers. . . .

Two Ways Hate-Speech Rules Could Be Drafted

Campus rules could be drafted either to prohibit expressions of racial hatred and contempt directly through a two-step approach, or to regulate behavior currently actionable in tort. In either case, the rules must be neutral and apply across the board, that is, must not single out particular forms of hateful speech for punishment while leaving others untouched. Moreover, any campus considering enacting such rules should be certain to compile adequate legislative evidence of their necessity.

The direct prohibition approach would couple two provisions. The first would prohibit face-to-face invective calculated seriously to disrupt the victim's ability to function in a campus setting. This provision, which must be race-neutral, could be tailored to capture the content of any recognized First Amendment exception, such as fighting words or workplace harassment. Because of the university's special role and responsibility for the safety and morale of students, even the precaution of working within a recognized exception might not be necessary. A second provision would provide enhanced punishment for any campus offense (including the one just described) which was proven to have been committed with a racial motivation. Such a two-step approach would satisfy all current constitutional requirements. It would promote a compelling and legitimate institutional interest. It would not single out particular types of expression, but rather particular types of motivation at the punishment stage. And it would not abridge rules against content or viewpoint neutrality, since it focuses not on the speaker's message but on its intended effect on the hearer, namely to impair his or her ability to function on campus.

Alternatively, a hate-speech rule could be patterned after an existing tort, such as intentional infliction of emotional distress or group libel, with the race of the victim a "special factor" calling for increased protection, as current rules . . . already provide. Tort law's neutrality and presumptive constitutionality strongly suggest that such an approach would be valid. . . . Harm-based rationales for punishing hate speech should be valid if the social injury from the speech outweighs its benefits.

Why Hate-Speech Rules Should Be Valid

The strongest reason for enacting hate-speech rules on campuses with a history of disruption is that they are necessary to promote equality. But even if one puts aside this consideration and views the controversy purely through the free speech lens, the policy concerns underlying our system of free expression are at best weakly promoted by protecting hate speech. Targeted racist vitriol scarcely advances self-government or the search for consensus. It does not promote the search for truth, nor help the speaker reach self-actualization, at least in any ideal sense. Racist speech thus does little to advance any of the theoretical rationales scholars and judges have advanced as reasons for protecting speech.

Looking at the hate-speech problem from the perspective of enforcement yields no greater support for the free-speech position. Our system distrusts any form of official speech regulation because we fear that the government will use the power to control the content of speech to insulate itself from criticism. This danger is absent, however, when the government sets out to regulate speech between private speakers, especially about subjects falling outside the realm of politics. When the government intervenes to tell one class of speakers to avoid saying hurtful things to another, governmental aggrandizement is at best a remote concern. This is the reason why regulation of private speech—libel, copyright, plagiarism, deceptive advertising, and so on—rarely presents serious constitutional problems. The same should be true of hate speech.

A Legitimate Case for Speech Codes

There is a legitimate case for universities prohibiting harassment of students on discriminatory grounds, grounds of race or sex. The case is roughly the same as the case for making harassment based on sex and race illegal in the workplace. . . .

The problem then is that harassment can be carried out by means of speech. So if you are going to prohibit harassment, you are going to regulate speech, and when you do that you create the danger of suppressing debate, suppressing ideas. My idea is that when that danger arises, we are better off making clear and defining in objective terms what speech can be regulated, what speech can count as harassment.

The alternative, which Alan Kors recommended, is simply to prohibit harassment and leave it to case-by-case determination what conduct shall fall under the prohibition. That's what the slogan "No Speech Codes" leads to—you can't specify in advance what kind of speech may count as harassment, can't specify it by content, because if you do that, you have written a speech code.

Thomas C. Grey, *Academic Questions*, Summer 1997.

Another political process concern is also absent. Our legal system resists speech regulation in part because of concern over selective regulation or enforcement. If the state were given the power to declare particular speakers disfavored, it could effectively exclude them from public discourse. We would forfeit the benefit of their ideas, while they would lose access to an important means for advancing their own interest. But none of these dangers is present with hate speech. Allowing the government to create a special offense for a class of persons (even racists) is indeed troublesome, as the Supreme Court recognized in *R.A.V. v. St. Paul.* But the direct prohibition approach we have outlined introduces the racial element only at the sentencing stage, where the dangers and political-process concerns of selective treatment are greatly reduced. The same would be true if the tort approach were adopted. In tort law, it is the intent and injury that matter, not the content of the speech. Enforcement comes from private initiative, not state action. Prevention of harm is the goal, with no speech disfavored as such.

But Will It Happen?

In the wake of recent cases, there is little reason today in First Amendment jurisprudence for leaving campus hate speech unregulated. Censorship and governmental nest-feathering are not implicated by rules against private speech. Nor does targeted racial vilification promote any of the theoretical rationales for protecting free speech. Much less does permissiveness toward racist name-calling benefit the victim, as the ACLU (American Civil Liberties Union) and others have argued. Far from acting as a pressure valve which enables rage to dissipate harmlessly, epithets increase their victims' vulnerability. Pernicious images create a world in which some come to see others as proper victims. Like farmyard chickens with a speck of blood, they may be reviled, mistreated, denied jobs, slighted, spoken of derisively, even beaten at will.

The Greeks used the term *hubris* to describe the sin of believing that one may "treat other people just as one pleases, with the arrogant confidence that one will escape any penalty for violating their rights." Those who tell ethnic jokes and hurl epithets are guilty of this kind of arrogance. But some who defend these practices, including First Amendment purists, are guilty as well: insisting on free speech over all, as though *no* countervailing interests were at stake, and putting forward transparently paternalistic justifications for a regime in which hate speech flows freely is also hubris. Unilateral power can beget arrogance, including the arrogance of insisting that one's worldview, one's interests, and one's way of framing an issue, are the only ones. Unfettered speech, a freemarket in which only some can prevail, is an exercise of power. Some words have no purpose other than to subordinate, injure, and wound. Free speech defenders insist that the current regime is necessary and virtuous, that minorities must acquiesce to this injurious and demeaning definition of virtue, and that their refusal to subordinate their interests to those of the First Amendment is evidence of their childlike simplicity and lack of insight into their own condition. These impositions may well be the greatest hubris of all.

In a hundred years, the hate-speech controversy may well come to be seen as the *Plessy v. Ferguson* of our age. In *Plessy*, the Supreme Court professed to be unable to see a moral difference between two claims—that of blacks to sit in a railroad car with whites, and that of whites to sit in a car without blacks. The hate-speech controversy features the same sort of perverse neutralism. The speaker claims a right to utter face-to-face racial invective. The victim insists he or she has the right not to have it spoken to him or her. A perfect standoff, just like the railroad car case, one right balanced against its perfect reciprocal.

Perhaps because scholars and policymakers realize the hollowness of the neutral principles approach and remember how poorly its predecessor fared in history's judgment, the weight of legal opinion has been slowly swinging in the direction of narrowly drawn hate-speech rules. Free speech traditionalists, focusing solely on one value and ignoring what else is at stake, have been fighting a holding action, using four paternalistic arguments for maintaining the status quo. These arguments each assert that even if hate-speech controls are constitutional, they are unwise because they would injure the very persons sought to be protected. Each of these arguments is invalid, a thin veneer, unsupported by empirical evidence, aimed at rationalizing the current regime.

Tinged with more than a little hubris, the liberals' arguments do not hold.

"[Censorship] represents a literal violation, an unwanted intrusion into the free spirit of individual people. It creates a hostile environment."

Campus Speech Codes Violate Free Speech

Jon Katz

Jon Katz is a scholar with the First Amendment Center who writes regularly on free speech issues. In the following viewpoint, Katz discusses two books that examine censorship and the increasing prevalence of speech codes on college campuses. Katz cites numerous examples of the use of hate speech restrictions to punish politically incorrect speech, and he notes that the courts have struck down these speech codes as unconstitutional. He contends that college campuses with speech codes resemble more the repressive regime of communist China than the freedom-loving United States.

As you read, consider the following questions:
1. What are the facts behind the "water buffalo case," as documented by Katz?
2. Who are the heroes in *The Shadow University*, according to the author?
3. How does Yale University differ from the other universities discussed by Kors and Silverglate, as cited by Katz?

Reprinted from "The New Censors: Part 2," by Jon Katz, *The Freedom Forum Online*, October 22, 1998, found at www.freedomforum.org/technology/1998/10/22katz.asp.

C ensorship has become comfortable to new constituen-
cies.

Minorities, liberals, boomer parents, feminists and aca-
demics are just as likely as Christian evangelists to be denouncing somebody for saying this, blocking that Web site
or boycotting this TV show, or forbidding the utterance of
that offensive thought.

Censorship Has Changed

In our time, the very context in which censorship occurs has
changed radically. Censors have always assumed themselves
to be acting out of moral, not censorious, concerns. The mo-
mentous change we face in the evolution of censorship,
writes essayist J.M. Coetzee in *Giving Offense*, is that while
state control of information has declined in South Africa,
Eastern Europe and much of Asia, the "liberal consensus on
freedom of expression that might once have been said to
reign among the Western intellectuals, and that indeed did
much to define them as a community, has ceased to obtain.
In the United States, for instance, institutions of learning
have approved bans on certain categories of speech, while
agitation against pornography is not limited to the right."

Nor, Coetzee might have added, are efforts to rate movies
and TV, punish films that don't conform to contemporary
political ideology, disconnect libraries from the Internet,
and put v-chips into TV sets. Censorship technology has become a booming business, helped along by morally oblivious
journalists spreading phobic notions about endangered children, and pandering politicians exploiting the anxieties of
the Information Revolution.

In the mid '80s, Coetzee writes, he could have assumed that
the "intelligentsia" shared his sentiment that the fewer legal
restraints there were on speech, the better. If it turned out that
some of the forms assumed by free speech were unfortunate,
even offensive, that was part of the price of freedom.

But that is not the ethos of '90s, which often equates sensitivity and freedom as parallel ideals, increasingly subordinating the latter to the former.

The idea that one has the right to be boorish, offensive or
obnoxious seems no longer widely accepted, even though it

was the point of the First Amendment—not to protect safe, but to protect unsafe, speech. Thus views seen as bigoted, culturally offensive, sexist, racist, homophobic or reactionary are not seen merely as wrong-headed notions to be criticized or challenged. In contemporary American culture—even in journalism and academe, where one would assume a reverence for the free exchange of ideas would be ingrained—"offensive" speech is not only not being tolerated, it is increasingly being severely punished, forbidden, sometimes even criminalized.

In 1995, a liberal baby boomer president supported and fought for the Communications Decency Act, a widely supported law that has more in common with apartheid controls on morality and decency than with American traditions of free speech.

Had the CDA been enacted into law, teen-age sexual discussions online would have become a federal crime, a trade-off that the solicitor general of the United States told the Supreme Court was a small price to pay for keeping Johnny off the *Playboy* Web site.

It's hard to believe the United States Congress would overwhelmingly support such legislation, or that a president who talks enthusiastically about preparing America for the new millennium would sign it.

The Shadow University

The new context of censorship in America is brilliantly, if horrifically, documented in a new book called *The Shadow University: The Betrayal of Liberty On America's Campuses*, by Alan Charles Kors, a professor of history at the University of Pennsylvania and the editor-in-chief of the *Oxford Encyclopedia of the Enlightenment*, and Harvey A. Silvergate, a former Harvard Law school professor, civil-liberties litigator and columnist for the *National Law Journal*.

The Shadow University is as shocking as it is meticulously documented. It details case after case in which universities have enacted blatantly unconstitutional speech and behavior codes, sought to punish conservative, politically incorrect, and other unfashionable thinking with arbitrary and draconian punishments including Maoist-like moral re-education

138

programs and Star Chamber legal proceedings that deny the most minimal elements of due process.

In the nation's best universities—places we assume would be bastions of liberty—students and professors are threatened with expulsion, suspicion and humiliation for boorish remarks, sometimes completely innocent and unintended.

Scores of federal court rulings tossing out university speech codes, overturning outrageously arbitrary and secret administrative judgments are blisteringly documented by Kors and Silverglate, whose damning indictment of the censorship culture in the country's supposedly most open arenas is all the more powerful for the fact that it is made by two obviously left-leaning civil libertarians.

The Water Buffalo Case

The most famous incident detailed in the book is the much-publicized case of a University of Pennsylvania student investigated by the campus police, hauled before a secret administrative board, and threatened with expulsion for yelling "water buffalo" out the window at a group of loudly partying minority women while he was trying to work.

The student said he never made the remark in any racial context, nor was there any evidence of any sort presented that he had. In fact, the water buffalo, it turns out, isn't even from Africa.

None of this stopped an Ivy League school from taking the very kind of social exchange that has characterized university life for centuries and threatening the student with disgrace and ruin. Only a barrage of unfavorable negative publicity made the school back down, and as Kors and Silverglate document so powerfully, there are hundreds, perhaps even thousands, of others who weren't or couldn't afford to be so brave.

There is little doubt, after reading this book, that this period in American university life will be viewed in the future in much the same way McCarthyism is viewed now in politics.

Other Outrageous Examples

Kors and Silverglate describe dozens of other equally outrageous examples—professors charged with harassment for mentioning explicitly sexual literature in class, or suspended for anonymous and unproven allegations by students. There are resident advisers (RAs) fired for refusing to wear badges that showed solidarity with gay rights, students and administrators forced into re-education classes, sometimes even therapy, for failing to show sensitivity to one oppressed group or another, and Orwellian speech and behavior codes tossed out by one shocked and outraged federal judge after another.

A Denial of Diversity

The [campus speech] codes, together with their accompanying "sensitivity training" and army of school administrators on the prowl for any signs of the suspect -isms, assign group identities to students and segregate them into the "weak" (needing protection) and the "strong" (requiring strict supervision). By assigning group identities and then according them special protection, the universities patronizingly assume that members of minority groups are so damaged by discrimination that they cannot speak for themselves. Furthermore, by assuming that there is such a thing as "the woman's viewpoint," "the gay/lesbian viewpoint," the politically correct orthodoxy denies diversity within minority communities.

Ben Lehrer, *Harvard Law Record*, vol. 108, no. 2 (1998).

Professors found themselves locked out of their own classrooms, forbidden to teach and denied all contact with their students as a result of secret accusations (the students were presumed too fragile ever to actually have to confront their abusers and harassers) that their teachings and behavior were creating "hostile" classroom environments.

Kors and Silverglate make an eerie but oddly convincing argument that the most oppressed minorities at America's best colleges in modern times are white, conservative and outspokenly religious men. White students have been banned from African-American residences and meeting facilities and forced to admit their innate racism and homophobia. One RA at Penn hid his deeply religious views on homosexuality until forced to admit them publicly at a "sensitivity" training session, after which he was promptly removed from his position and ordered to undergo re-education. He won his job back in court.

Universities have had to settle hundreds of outrageous and stupid cases like that one, report Kors and Silverglate, but almost always insisting on secrecy agreements, so that few of them become public.

Conservative newspapers are routinely burned, removed, vandalized or destroyed without a single student ever having been known to be punished for doing these things. Politically incorrect pamphlets are defaced or torn from bulletin boards.

Institutions that are supposed to be breeding grounds for original and innovative thought have embraced the forced re-ordering of moral conscience.

Smith College announced that students and faculty guilty of committing incidents that "dishonor cultural identity" would be offered channels for "education, reintegration and forgiveness."

Beyond Belief

The speech codes instituted at colleges and universities and detailed by Kors and Silverglate would be almost beyond belief if they weren't so commonplace.

Bowdoin College prohibits stories "experienced by others as harassing." Brown University prohibits speech that produces "feelings of impotence," "anger" or "disenfranchisement," intentional or unintentional. Colby College bans speech that causes "loss of self-esteem" or a "vague sense of danger." The code of the University of Vermont demands that "each of us must assume responsibility for becoming educated about racism, sexism, ageism, homophobia/heterosexism, and other forms of oppression. . . ."

Sarah Lawrence College found a student guilty of harassment for "laughing" when he heard another student call a young man, a former roommate with whom he had feuded, a "faggot." Without being permitted to confront his accuser, the student who laughed and the one who used the term were found guilty of creating a "hostile and intimidating atmosphere" and sentenced to one year's social probation and 20 hours of community service.

Furthermore, the school required both of the "offending" students to view a videotape called "Homophobia," read a publication, *Homophobia on Campus*, and write a paper on homophobia.

One RA who didn't want to watch a sexually explicit film on gay life because of his religious convictions lost his position. The University of Maryland-College Park lists among "unacceptable verbal behaviors . . . idle chatter of a sexual nature," "graphic sexual descriptions; sexual slurs, sexual innuendos," "comments about a person's clothing, body, and/or sexual activities," "sexual teasing," "suggestive or insulting sounds such as whistling, wolf-calls, or kissing sounds," "sexually provocative compliments about a person's clothes," "comments of a sexual nature about weight, body shape, size or figure," "comments or questions about the sensuality of a person, or his/her spouse or significant other," "pseudo-medical advice such as 'You might be feeling bad because you didn't get enough' or 'A little Tender Loving Care (TLC) will cure your ailments,'" "telephone calls of a sexual nature," "stage whispers" or "mimicking of a sexual nature about the way a person walks, talks [or] sits." Furthermore, said the university, to constitute harassment these remarks don't necessarily have to be directed at a specific individual. They can simply be uttered out loud.

Reminiscent of Maoist China

Many of these schools have created bizarre, secret, but powerful internal cultural law enforcement apparatuses to enforce speech and behavior codes—Diversity Response Teams, Multi-Cultural Response Units, Sensitivity Officers, Equal Opportunity enforcement investigators.

Without the consistent intervention of incredulous federal courts, some of America's best schools would more closely resemble Maoist China during the Cultural Revolution than places where people pay a fortune to learn how to think and reason.

Kors and Silverglate list speech code after speech code, region by region, outrage after outrage, presented in convincing, detailed, or overwhelming context. Parents thinking of sending their kids to college will tremble at reading how the people running some of these schools actually think.

This book is as depressing as it is riveting, mostly because it shows us how the best and brightest among us so easily gather into herds and subvert notions of freedom, privacy, dignity and common sense.

There are few heroes in *The Shadow University* apart from the handful of courageous students and professors who risked their jobs, academic standing and futures to challenge their schools and their proceedings in court.

And it's striking how few colleges and universities even considered notions like the First Amendment, which posits that the right to free speech is a seminal freedom in the United States, even—perhaps especially—when it provokes and offends.

In 1975, Yale University rejected the kinds of codes and policies being adopted by many other schools. Yale said it embraced "unfettered freedom, the right to think the un-thinkable, discuss the unmentionable, and challenge the un-challengeable." It explicitly rejected the notion that "soli-darity," "harmony," "civility" or "mutual respect" could be higher values than free expression at a university.

Even when individual students fail to meet their social and ethical responsibilities, Yale promised, the paramount obliga-tion of the university is to protect their right to free expression.

"Contrary to the expectations of most applicants, colleges and universities are not freer than the society at large," write Kors and Silverglate. "Indeed, they are less free, and that diminution is continuing apace. In a nation whose future de-pends upon an education in freedom, college and universi-ties are teaching the values of censorship, self-censorship, and self-righteous abuse of power."

Universities, say Kors and Silverglate in perhaps the most jolting sentence in this book, have become "enemies of a free society."

The Shadow University is not happy reading for anybody who believes in the free movement of ideas and discussion.

New Kinds of Censors

It echoes and reinforces Coetzee's observation that the new context of censorship in America is that many of the people who have always most vigorously opposed it—liberals, aca-demics, intellectuals, journalists—have become new kinds of censors in their own right, people for whom freedom has dropped down some notches on the list of social priorities.

Journalists are as apt to be listing toll-free numbers to call for blocking software [filters that block out pornography on the Internet] as they are to be challenging it. Intellectuals are as likely to be forcing particular notions of sensitivity, morality and sensitivity on individuals as they are to be defending freedom and individual moral choice.

The word censorship is used so often, and in so many different and reflexive ways, that it has lost much of its real meaning and power. We have more information available to us than ever before, and, it seems, more people trying to curb or ban much of it. We never seem to get to a comfortable or permanent place with censorship. We never quite find a balance or reach consensus.

We Are All Censors

Although we always tend to see censors as Others, we are all censors at different points in our lives, sometimes for good and necessary reasons. Consider the parent who forbids a child to speak rudely, the state legislature that forbids the filing of false reports. Nearly everyone who works for someone else censors himself or herself at one point or another, and there are many things we wouldn't—shouldn't—say to friends, family members or colleagues.

Yet in these times, with the collapse of so many noxious political systems and the spread of so much obnoxious information and imagery, it's sometimes possible to forget that censorship is a repugnant, degrading and thoroughly discredited idea in the 20th Century.

Ultimately, it has failed almost everywhere it has been applied, no matter how vigorously and viciously. Because most Americans have never experienced institutionalized censorship in the way Coetzee and [Soviet dissident author Aleksandr] Solzhenitsyn and millions of others have, we seem to have developed a relatively low consciousness of it and a growing tolerance for its more subtle forms.

Respectable moderates rarely need to have their speech protected; they don't say or write things that anger people or governments. Nor do the consciously sensitive or politically correct. It's the Larry Flynts of the world for whom the First Amendment was created [Flynt is publisher of *Hustler* magazine].

144

Offensive Speech Is Entitled to Protection

For the first time in the history of the world, a government—18th Century America's—advanced the idea that unpopular, even offensive speech was entitled to protection, an idea that seems endangered even in the very places that are supposed to teach it.

How odd that in our time, governments are censoring free speech and popular culture less in the name of order and preserving virtue, and our so-called intelligentsia are curbing it more frequently because it sometimes gives offense.

For me, censorship is personal. It represents a literal violation, an unwanted intrusion into the free spirit of individual people. It creates a hostile environment.

Looking around at our own society, supposedly the freest on the planet, we might be wise to keep J.M. Coetzee's description of the censor in our wallets, above our bathroom mirrors, or posted above our computers:

"The one who pronounces the ban . . . becomes, in effect, the blind one, the one at the center of the ring in the game of blind man's bluff."

Periodical Bibliography

The following articles have been selected to supplement the diverse views presented in this chapter. Addresses are provided for periodicals not indexed in the *Readers' Guide to Periodical Literature*, the *Alternative Press Index*, the *Social Sciences Index*, or the *Index to Legal Periodicals and Books*.

Dudley Barlow	"Teaching Core Democratic Values?" *Education Digest*, January 2000.
Judy Blume	"Is Harry Potter Evil?" *The New York Times*, October 22, 1999.
Liz Featherstone	"Free Speech: Look Who's Flunking," *Columbia Journalism Review*, July/August 1999.
David Keim	"Parents Push for Wizard-Free Reading," *Christianity Today*, January 10, 2000.
Ross Kerber	"Kids Say the Darnedest Things," *Wall Street Journal*, November 17, 1997.
Skip Lowery	"Censorship: Tactics for Defense," *Phi Delta Kappan*, March 1998.
Terry McManus	"Home Web Sites Thrust Students into Censorship Disputes," *The New York Times*, August 13, 1998.
Barbara Miner	"Reading, Writing, and Censorship," *Rethinking Schools*, Spring 1998.
Peggy Orenstein	"Censorship Follies, Town by Town," *The New York Times*, December 7, 1996.
Susan Philips	"Student Journalism," *CQ Researcher*, June 5, 1998.
Robert Riehemann	"Family Friendly Libraries," *Free Inquiry*, Spring 1997. Available from the Council for Secular Humanism, PO Box 664, Amherst, NY 14226.

CHAPTER 4

Should the Arts and Entertainment Industries Be Censored?

Chapter Preface

The name of the art exhibit, "Sensation," sponsored by the Brooklyn Museum of Art in the fall of 1999 was apt—it did cause a sensation, not just in New York, but across the entire country. The exhibit contained several pieces of controversial art, the most well known of which was Chris Orfili's "Holy Virgin Mary," a portrait of a black Virgin Mary decorated with elephant dung and pornographic photos. Rudolph Giuliani, the mayor of New York, was so disgusted by the "sick stuff" in the exhibit that he refused to pay the city's $500,000 monthly subsidy to the museum unless it cancelled the exhibit.

Giuliani contends that artists are free to create offensive work such as "Holy Virgin Mary," "but to have the government subsidize something like that is outrageous." Furthermore, he believes the Orfili portrait is an example of "Catholic bashing," a type of hate speech specifically meant to offend Roman Catholics. "If this were a desecration of a symbol in another area, I think there would be more sensitivity about this than a desecration of a symbol that involves Catholics," he asserted.

Critics of Giuliani argue that his efforts to shut down the exhibit are censorship and a violation of the First Amendment. They note that the First Amendment protects the expression of unpopular ideas and prohibits government from suppressing them. Critics cite the Supreme Court's decision in *NEA v. Finley*, which found that although the government has no obligation to finance art, once it does, it has no right to impose "a penalty on disfavored viewpoints."

Every few years, a new controversy erupts over government funding of the arts. The viewpoints in the following chapter explore this issue as well as the question of whether the entertainment media should be censored.

"Those . . . who consider the influence of the mass media to be malignant . . . will seek some recourse. Censorship . . . is that recourse."

The Entertainment Industry Should Be Censored

David Lowenthal

David Lowenthal teaches political science at Assumption College and Boston College and is the author of *No Liberty for License: The Forgotten Logic of the First Amendment.* In the following viewpoint, Lowenthal argues that the mass media—the film, television, and music industries—are responsible for the decline of American society. Since the sex and violence portrayed by the mass media have become more explicit over the years, it is obvious that the industry is incapable of censoring itself. Therefore, Lowenthal asserts, the government must step in and censor the mass media to prevent the total destruction of society.

As you read, consider the following questions:

1. On what four premises does Lowenthal base his argument for why the mass media must be censored?
2. According to Lowenthal, what concerns are conservatives and liberals especially sensitive to?
3. Who does the author believe should censor the entertainment industry, and how would their decisions be made?

Excerpted from "Why the Mass Media Must Be Censored," by David Lowenthal, *Jurist*, October 1998. Reprinted with permission from the author.

The argument [for why the mass media must be censored] rests on these premises: (1) that the mass media are the prime educational force in the country; (2) that their effect is, by and large, pernicious—running counter to the education of the young in schools, churches and synagogues, and to the qualities required of mature citizens in a civilized republic; (3) that the brutes, lechers and slobs the media tend to produce will have no aptitude for or love of republican government; (4) that government, and government alone, has a chance of blocking this descent into decadence. The argument to be overcome is that censorship is dangerous, ineffective, unconstitutional, and inconsistent with liberal democracy.

By "mass media," I mean television, the movies, and recordings primarily, but the term can be extended to cover cheap books and magazines, and now the Internet as well. For present purposes, I shall concentrate on the first three media. There are few people in the country insensitive enough to regard television and the movies as mere entertainment, but there are some. Their view is that what we see and hear with such frequency is like water off a peach or a duck's back: We are amused, moved, or entranced without being affected or changed. Censorship is not for them. Those, however, who consider the influence of the mass media to be malignant—and some have likened it to a moral sewer—will seek some recourse. Censorship—or, more broadly, regulation—is that recourse.

Should We Worry?

As a nation, we are concerned about pollution, about pure air and water, about every aspect of the physical environment, about the prevention and cure of disease in all its forms. Is there no such thing as moral pollution? Has our increasing awareness of the goods and evils of the body been bought at the cost of an increasing stupefaction regarding the goods and evils of the soul? Are we incapable of recognizing the debilitation of the soul that weakens or destroys those qualities that make us distinctively human?

That there is cause for concern about the media is recognized by thoughtful conservatives and liberals alike. Conservatives are especially sensitive to the sexual immorality the media convey, liberals to the encouragement given to violence. Both are right, but the picture is much more alarming than even the combination of the two. Never before in the whole history of mankind have the moral restraints and aspirations necessary to the fullness of our nature, and to civilization itself, been subjected to so ubiquitous and persistent an assault. If our scientific learning and partisan ideologies keep us from seeing this—from seeing that we are on the road to decadence and decline—of what use are they? . . .

How can we expect the sexes to treat each other with decency and respect, the very young to forbear from sexual intercourse, and the family to remain stable in mutual devotion if the joys of sex, unrelated to any sense of responsibility and separated even from love, are touted daily in theaters and on television screens? Is it unreasonable to believe that an important cause of the instability of the American family today, and of our enormous rate of illegitimacy, is the climate of sexual laxity produced by movie after movie, show after show? . . .

A Little History

Obscenity has never been protected by the First Amendment, though today we have sunk so low that some people, no doubt thinking of themselves as progressive revolutionaries, have begun to argue that pornography itself—the most primitive form of obscenity—should have the shroud of unconstitutionality lifted from it.

We need not review all the changes that the Supreme Court has made in the law of obscenity, starting in 1957. Suffice it to say that the result has been to discourage the prosecution of obscenity by narrowing its legal definition to sheer pornography, so that all those appeals to lust short of the exhibition of sexual organs and acts can no longer be considered illegal. Even the prosecution of pornography has been rendered dispirited, as if out of fashion in a more progressive age.

In recent years, the Court has gone so far as to insist that "indecency" be given its share of viewing hours on television, and that the Internet be left an unregulated realm of freedom (despite extremely worrisome elements such as pornography, instructions in bomb production and sexual luring that have already shown themselves there). A single instance of how the Court's 1973 obscenity decision in *Miller v. California* works in action tells it all. In the lower courts, the lyrics of the rap group *2 Live Crew* were given First Amendment protection. This occurred because of courtroom testimonials to their "serious value" by so-called experts, despite the fact that they manifestly contain obscenity, indecency, and the provocation of violence to women altogether.

You don't have to be [conservative columnist] George Will, or a member of the Christian Right, to realize that something is radically wrong. If we want a capsule formulation, the Supreme Court, the law schools, and part of the country have replaced the thought of the founders and framers with ideas derived from John Stuart Mill's extreme philosophy of liberty, mixed incoherently with the morally corroding relativism of mid-twentieth century thought. Pressed by secular intellectuals to liberate ourselves from Victorian and Puritan prudery, we have thrown off all restraints, thinking we can satisfy all natural appetites while remaining civilized and free.

The mass media—movies, television and recordings—need to be regulated, and not only because of appeals to irresponsible lust. They have immersed us in violence as well, habituated us to it in its most extreme forms, held it up as a model where it shouldn't be, and surrounded us by images of hateful human types so memorable as to cause a psychological insecurity that is unhealthy and dangerous. The only answer is governmental regulation, if necessary prior to publication—that is, censorship. As to the possibility of self-regulation by the industries involved, the case of the movies is proof enough that this cannot work. The profit motive, left to itself, will not serve the common good.

Meeting Objections

I must now face these questions: (1) Is not prior restraint or censorship in the strict sense banned by the very idea of the "freedom of the press"? Would censorship of the movies and the other mass media we are considering be constitutional? (2) Can censorship be made responsible and consistent with the needs of republican government? Why should what we see and hear be determined by some faceless bureaucrats? Will censorship not be misused and abused by politicians? (3) Is censorship enough to correct the moral corruption that has already shown itself in our midst?

An Advocate for Censorship

Christianity Today advisory editor Michael Cromartie visited with Robert H. Bork in his Washington office at the American Enterprise Institute, where Bork is the John H. Olin Scholar in Legal Studies. . . .

CT: *You write that "Sooner or later censorship is going to have to be considered as popular culture continues plunging to ever more sickening lows." Are you advocating censorship?*

Yes.

CT: *What fine distinctions do you make?*

I don't make any fine distinctions; I'm just advocating censorship. It's odd that we've grown so sensitive about the topic of censorship that if somebody mentions it everybody begins to shake all over and say, "Oh my! That's an unthinkable thought." We had censorship in this country up until the last couple of decades. Almost all of our national existence we had censorship. When I was practicing law in Chicago as a young lawyer, the city of Chicago had a censorship board for movies. It didn't suppress any good art, it didn't eliminate any ideas; but it did keep a certain amount of filth out of the theaters.

CT: *How would this censorship actually work?*

We don't have to guess how censorship would work; we've seen it work. It's just like any other law. You get the elected representatives to write a code about what is obscene and can be prohibited, and then an executive branch official applies the code to some instance. If the person involved thinks the code has been misapplied, or that the code itself is defective, he goes to the courts for relief.

Robert H. Bork, interviewed by Michael Cromartie, *Christianity Today*, May 19, 1997.

It is true that "freedom of the press" originally meant the end of censorship, but it was "the press"—the production of books, pamphlets, handbills—that was freed because its abuses could be corrected by legal punishment subsequent to publication. The movies, television, recordings, and the

Internet are entirely different from the press in this respect. They can be "published" at once all over the country, distributed to young and old alike. That is why they are called the *mass* media. Furthermore, their visual and sound appeals, embodied in drama and music, give them a power totally different from that of the "press" in the old and exact sense. Likening or assimilating them to the press, thus understood, is like calling atomic missiles artillery.

We cannot be sure that the first stout defenders of the press, such as William Blackstone or John Milton—both of whom favored subsequent punishment for abuses of the press—would make an exception for the movies and television were they alive today. But their principle would require it, for they presume that serious harm to the public by the use of words or pictures is to be prohibited, so that the choice of how to do so, while important, is still a secondary consideration. Preventing harm coming from printed materials could be accomplished after publication, but with movies and television the harm from even a single showing can be widespread, deep, and not easily overcome.

Constitutional Tradition

As to our own constitutional tradition, the Supreme Court has never closed the door to prior restraint in the case of movies, realizing that they constitute a new and unique medium. In fact, as far back as 1931 (in *Near v. Minnesota*), even before movies became a powerful force, Chief Justice Charles Hughes stated, as a matter of course, that there were four specific abuses of the press in connection with which the First Amendment would allow even prior restraint (i.e., censorship). One of the four was that "the primary requirements of decency may be enforced against obscene publications."

The case of television is different because, like radio, stations or bends of airwaves are a public property allocated with conditions attached. In the Federal Communications Act of 1934, it was stipulated that programming had to be in the "public interest"—a basic condition Congress failed to amplify upon then or since. But the principle is there, ready to be made more specific in the future. If the conditions for obtaining and renewing licenses are made plain and then applied consistently, there should be little need for the prior screening of individual programs.

Who Will Censor?

Who will do the censoring? In monarchical days of old, it was an individual appointed by the King from whose secret decisions there was no appeal. In our own experience, only a few years ago there were boards of censors as well as individual censors in many of our states and cities, driven out of existence not by being considered unconstitutional as such but by the increasing restrictions placed on them by the Supreme Court. In 1959, for example, a case came before the Court (*Kingsley International Picture Corporation v. Regents*) involving the refusal of the Board of Regents of that state to allow the showing of the movie, *Lady Chatterley's Lover*. In those days, the individuals involved were often appointed and relatively unknown, but it would be possible to find ways of getting some of our most distinguished citizens to serve as censors, now that we realize (as before we did not) how central, rather than peripheral, this function really is. In our almost fastidious legal system, their decisions—unlike those of the censors of old—would be guided by law, open to inspection, and subject to review by higher courts. Can this power be abused? Of course it can, but the much greater danger is that its power, rightly exercised, will be eluded by the horde of innovators now thrusting their products on an unwitting public.

A More Important Question

A more important question is whether enough is left of our moral character and understanding as a nation to be able to frame and apply laws that will control the most baneful aspects of the mass media. No one knows. It is easy to be deceived by what we see on television, which is hardly capable of peering into the urban and rural heartlands of America. And, while there are other sources of our moral corruption— including excessive wealth—the mass media, by creating the world of ideas and images with which we picture ourselves, are the most obvious and most important. A sick man is often helped through his illness by his will to prevail, and by the measures taken to make him well. Having recourse to a reasonable but rigorous system of censorship will signify that the country understands what has happened and is determined to survive as a civilized and free society.

As for the final complaint—"I don't want anybody telling me what I can or can't see"—the answer is simple. That is exactly our situation now, where completely hidden figures in movie studios and television networks, often only a few, and motivated primarily by profit, decide what will be available for our viewing. With few exceptions, the choice the viewer has is usually from a variety of bad alternatives, whatever their technical wizardry. For inch-by-inch and yard-by-yard, the mass media have lowered the standards of their productions, increasingly appealing to animal appetites that, once released, care little for the nobler elements of freedom and civilization.

The choice is clear: either a rigorous censorship of the mass media, molded into responsible republican form, with censors known to all and operating under law, or an accelerating descent into barbarism and the destruction, sooner or later, of free society itself.

"Since the government won't tell us what we can't do, we have to tell ourselves what we can't do."

The Entertainment Industry Should Practice Self-Censorship

Michael D. Eisner

Michael D. Eisner is the chairman and chief executive officer of the Walt Disney Company. In the following viewpoint, which is an adaptation of a speech he gave in March 1998 to the American Society of Newspaper Editors, Eisner argues that simply because the government is forbidden by the First Amendment from practicing censorship, this does not mean the arts, news, and entertainment industries should produce vile and offensive programs, music, and other products. He asserts that these industries should take the responsibility of censoring themselves to ensure that the entertainment they produce is in good taste.

As you read, consider the following questions:

1. How is the First Amendment different from other legal documents, according to Eisner?
2. What examples does the author provide of media content that is permissible but undesirable if society wants to be civilized?
3. What type of entertainment product is valued in the long term, according to the author?

No matter how many times the First Amendment is quoted, there is a key aspect of it that is consistently overlooked, one that is especially important to everyone who works in news and entertainment: namely, the First Amendment doesn't apply to us.

A Passive Role

Of course, we are all direct beneficiaries of the First Amendment. But our role is passive. It all goes back to those first words, "Congress shall make no law . . ." In other words, it is setting rules of behavior for the government, not for us. This makes the amendment all the more remarkable.

After all, most legal documents dictate the behavior of citizens, instructing us on everything from how to drive our cars to how to build our homes to how to pay our taxes to even how to protect corporate trademarks with large round ears. The First Amendment does just the opposite; it regulates the government and lets us be.

This puts the U.S. in stark contrast to most other nations. Consider the words of Nelba Blandon, who directed Nicaragua's Office of Mass Media a decade ago. Here's what she had to say about the editorial content of *La Prensa*, Nicaragua's preeminent newspaper: "They accused us of suppressing freedom of expression. This was a lie and we could not let them publish it."

Nothing like that faces us here. Consider my own personal experience. For three decades—moving from TV shows to movies to theme parks—I've been involved in producing mediocre entertainment, good entertainment, occasionally great entertainment and sometimes even important entertainment.

Self-Serving Behavior

At Paramount, we made "Reds," which was about the communist John Reed. At Disney, we made "Blaze," about Louisiana Gov. Earl Long, and we made "Nixon," about, well . . . Nixon. Never once did I think, "What will the president think?" or "What will a governor think?" or, "What will a mayor or city council think?" I say this not because I am fearless but because the First Amendment gives me nothing to fear.

What I do think about is how we in the media sometimes conveniently embrace the First Amendment. How many times have you seen entertainment executives justify the release of vile programs and repugnant lyrics by sanctimoniously proclaiming "freedom of speech"?

This same self-serving behavior can be seen in the newspaper business. Certain publishers will print egregious material and then eagerly hide behind the skirts of the Constitution, saying, in effect, "The First Amendment made me do it."

© Ismael Roldan. Reprinted with permission.

Because the First Amendment does regulate the government, it has made our jobs much easier. But at the same time we have to make some tough choices. We all have to be editors—journalists and entertainers alike. Since the government won't tell us what we can't do, we have to tell ourselves what we can't do.

For example, last year Disney recalled an album because we found the lyrics offensive. Because we're far from perfect, the album did get recorded, and it did get released. When one of our executives brought the offensive lyrics to our attention, we took what we felt was the appropriate action.

Then there's a certain television show you may have heard of that we decided to keep on the air, despite the fact that its star walked publicly out of the closet. Given all the controversy, it would have been very easy for The Walt Disney Company to simply walk away from the show. But we didn't for a very simple reason: "Ellen" was a good show—it was well-written and intelligent, and (no small matter when it comes to a situation comedy) it was actually funny. In other words, our most controversial show passed the same test as arguably our least controversial show, "Home Improvement."

Free Speech Versus Responsibility

There is a constant tension between allowing artists who work for us to have the right to free expression and exercising our personal responsibility regarding the content of the product we put out. But edit we must—not to stifle conflict or conviction but to eliminate debasement. What I am talking about is good taste and good judgment.

Almost any subject can be dealt with tastefully in entertainment or in news—and almost any subject can be dealt with in ways that demean. Done well, all sorts of issues are worthy of exploration. But there *is* a boundary line—and generally we all know where it is—beyond which fantasy and adventure and escape turn into irresponsible depiction and inappropriate behavior. Profits do not excuse unethical decisions.

Citizens fighting like hockey players on television over sexual infidelities and worse; disk jockeys who make·racial and incendiary comments and more; rock groups advocating violence against women and police—these are permissible under the First Amendment. But they are not desirable if we aspire to call ourselves civilized.

Of course, the pressures are great to just join in. In all our businesses, a race to the bottom seems to be gaining momentum. But I believe that most of us want to head in a different direction. This is because we find that it is the high road that tends to take us to the best destinations, while the low road often leads to a dead end. We all take detours, at times, traveling toward the dark rather than the light. I believe in the light.

Primal Instincts

We are part of the civilized world, or at least we are supposed to be. We separate ourselves from the rest of the animal world by learning manners and poise and suppressing our primal instincts. And if all we do in creating our entertainment products is feed those suppressed desires, we will simply encourage barbarism. From "Schindler's List," to "60 Minutes," to "Scinfeld," to "Beauty and the Beast," it is work of quality and honor that is valued in the long term.

In the end, when we find ourselves on our deathbeds, I don't think we will say to our adoring family hovering nearby, "Do you remember that really salacious nude roller skater I put on the air back in '98? Wasn't that great television?" And I don't think our adoring spouses will smile and say, "Yes dear, that was [explctive deleted] wonderful."

> *"Curbing new ideas hurts not only individual creators but the audience for which they create and the posterity that inherits their legacy."*

The Entertainment Industry Should Not Be Censored

Virginia Postrel

Congress periodically holds hearings to question those in the entertainment industry about the amount of sex and violence in their films, music, and games, threatening to impose censorship if they do not regulate themselves. In the following viewpoint, Virginia Postrel argues against such calls for censorship. She notes that criteria for censorship are subjective; what one person considers objectionable another may believe is worth keeping. Furthermore, she maintains that if artists are censored—self-imposed or otherwise—who knows what masterpieces will be lost to society? Postrel is editor of *Reason*, a libertarian magazine.

As you read, consider the following questions:
1. Why did the English parliament close the playhouses in 1642, as cited by the author?
2. According to Postrel, how is the Clinton administration attempting to eliminate products from the marketplace?
3. Why does society have to put up with a certain number of bad cultural products, according to the author?

Whereas the distracted state of England, threatened with a cloud of blood by a civil war, calls for all possible means to appease and avert the wrath of God, it is therefore thought fit and ordained by the Lords and Commons in this parliament assembled that, while these set causes and set times of humiliation continue, public stage plays shall cease and be forborne.

—Parliamentary edict, September 2, 1642

In the United States, Congress does not close the playhouses. It just holds periodic hearings to bully the people who produce popular entertainment. They bow and scrape and halfheartedly apologize for their audience-pleasing products, usually by vague reference to unnamed works that go too far. Then everyone goes back to their business until the next time a committee chair decides the nation's distracted state warrants an attack on its favorite arts.

Entertainment as Demon

All of which happened, pretty much according to script, in response to the murders in Colorado. [In April 1999, two teens shot and killed twelve students and one teacher in their high school near Denver and then killed themselves.] The Senate Commerce Committee convened its show trial in early May 1999. The agenda was to make popular art into the equivalent of cigarettes: a demon drug sold by greedy liars to corrupt our youth. "Joe Camel has, sadly, not gone away," said Sen. Joseph Lieberman (R-Conn.), the committee's most eager attacker. "He's gone into the entertainment business."

Bill Bennett, described as "the conscience of America" by committee Chairman John McCain (R-Ariz.), came prepared to name works deserving censure, and possibly censorship. He showed clips from *Scream* and *The Basketball Diaries*. "Can you not distinguish between *Casino* and *Macbeth*, or *Casino* and *Braveheart*, or *The Basketball Diaries* and *Clear and Present Danger*?" Bennett said. "I can make that distinction."

Despite some chilling moments, the hearings flopped. Executives from the movie studios and record companies declined to come and cooperate in their own denunciation. Deprived of dramatic confrontations or lying CEOs, reporters and the nation yawned. A month later, the House soundly defeated two bills to regulate entertainment products—one through outright bans, another through cigarette-style labeling. A significant, bipartisan majority disagreed with Bennett that "in the matter of the protection of our children, nothing is off limits."

Not so the Clinton administration. It acted unilaterally to appease the soccer-mom gods. Adopting the tobacco model, the president ordered the Federal Trade Commission to investigate "whether and how video game, motion picture and recording industries market to children violent and other material rated for adults." The commission will exercise de facto subpoena power, demanding proprietary memos, private e-mail, and internal marketing studies. The attack on Hollywood is now part of the Clintonite campaign to restore the FTC's pre-Reagan punch; the issue is not free speech but free markets. The president is embracing Bennett's belief that "this is predatory capitalism."

If you want to eliminate a product from the American marketplace, this is the way you do it—not by act of Congress, but through administrative agencies helped along by liability suits. Clinton has unleashed the regulators, and the lawsuits have begun.

But what does it matter? Suppose all violent movies vanish from the theaters, made uneconomic by regulatory burdens, unpredictable lawsuits, and congressional harassment. Who cares?

The Subjectivity of Distinctions

The audience, for starters. Tens of millions of people saw *The Matrix*, a blockbuster hit and one of the recent movies most often attacked as a blight on our culture. Most of those moviegoers, including me, think *The Matrix* is a fine film whose existence is a positive good. It is visually striking, well acted, and intelligently written. It explores classic themes, arguing that it is better to face reality and struggle for freedom than to accept comfortable slavery and live in illusion. It is not Great Art, but it is good art, and good entertainment. We, its paying audience, would not want to see it destroyed.

This raises the problem that so annoys Bennett: the subjectivity of distinctions. Any objective standard that would censor *The Matrix* (or *Casino*) as too violent would have to curb *Macbeth* and *Braveheart* as well. Shakespeare's Scottish play is horrifyingly violent—Akira Kurosawa's retelling is aptly called *Throne of Blood*—and so is Mel Gibson's Scottish movie. *Braveheart* depicts torture and celebrates warfare. You cannot ban *Scream*, *The Matrix*, and *Casino* and make an exception for Bill Bennett's bloody favorites. The distinctions required are too fine, and a different critic would cut things differently.

I do sympathize with Bennett on one point: It is tiresome and clichéd to keep invoking Shakespeare, whom no one would dare ban today. But there's a reason the Bard keeps coming up, and it isn't that everyone in *Hamlet* ends up dead.

Sacrificing Individual Responsibility

Bad programming, says David Lowenthal, spews costs on third parties like so much car exhaust. Robert H. Bork attacks the "libertarian virus" that infects "free market economists . . . [who] ignore the question of which wants it is moral to satisfy."

Such claims are simply incorrect; to suggest that ordering up an adult flick on pay per view harms innocent third persons is nonsense. And free market economists are quite explicit about their belief in "consumer sovereignty." That is, individuals should be free to decide what they consume so long as that consumption does not require the curtailment of another's freedom. Strangely, Lowenthal and Bork deliver conservatives to the altar of collectivism, upon which they sacrifice individual responsibility.

Thomas W. Hazlett, *Reason*, November 1999.

That reason is seared in the consciousness of every English-language player, right down to the members of the Screen Actors Guild: You *can* ban Shakespeare. It happened. In 1642, the greatest period of English theater was ended by an act of Parliament. The milieu that had produced Shakespeare, and that continued to perform his plays, was destroyed. Those theaters were full of sex, violence, and special effects—and of poetry, ideas, and creative promise. English drama never fully recovered from the loss. Had the closure come a mere 50 years earlier, we would have lost *Romeo and Juliet* and everything that followed.

Loss and near loss haunt *Shakespeare in Love*, Hollywood's fondest vision of itself and its art. A Puritan preacher appears early on, denouncing the theaters as "the devil's handmaidens," and the authorities are always closing the playhouses. *Romeo and Juliet* barely finds a stage. "I would exchange all my plays to come for his that will never come," says Will Shakespeare when Kit Marlowe is killed. We modern moviegoers are presumed to know better. But it is not that easy a call. Marlowe's small oeuvre is extraordinary, all written before he was 30. Who knows what might have been his *Hamlet*?

The Heart of the Argument

Loss is at the heart of the argument against regulating creativity, whether in art, technology, or enterprise. The innovative process is a fragile one, dependent on a complex, often messy interplay of imagination, competition, and exchange. Curbing new ideas hurts not only individual creators but the audience for which they create and the posterity that inherits their legacy. Regulators destroy some goods directly, and we can count the cost. Other losses, like Marlowe's never-written plays, we can only imagine.

This is not simply a matter of great work but of the milieu from which it springs. To get the good stuff, you have to put up with the experiments that fail and the junk produced to pay the bills. Alongside the hack work of Greene and Dekker, even Shakespeare wrote some dogs. But crush *Titus Andronicus*, and you will lose *King Lear*. The same process produced them both.

How does it matter that in the 15th century China turned its back on exploration and innovation, that the world's most technologically creative nation became a backwater by decree? We cannot know for sure. But the loss, to the Chinese people and to the world, was surely significant.

When congressional pressure and anti-competitive opportunism created the Comics Code, declaring American comic books an inherently childish medium, EC Comics was destroyed and its readers bereft. That was the short-term effect. The larger loss was in the stories untold, the techniques unexplored. We can infer something of its magnitude by looking at the development of graphic story-telling in Europe and Japan. But we can never know what might have been.

Creativity Is a Social Good

In *The Future and Its Enemies*, I argue that individual creativity and enterprise are not only personally satisfying but socially good, producing progress and happiness. For celebrating creativity and happiness, I have been called a fascist by critics on both coasts. It is a peculiar charge, since fascism entails subordinating the individual to the nation—hardly a recipe for either self-expression or joy. But the charge expresses a coherent worldview, one that imagines freedom as the will to power and the good life as docile obedience.

This view quite naturally leads to crusades against popular art, particularly American art, since our native culture is anti-authority. Writing in *The American Spectator*, movie critic James Bowman denounces *The Matrix*, whose science fiction setting he clearly does not understand, for teaching "kids contempt for the values of work and sobriety and conformity to social norms." This critique condemns not just the movie but the inventiveness that made it possible. It is a prescription for the death of creativity and an attack on the American spirit. By this standard, *Hamlet* is safe. But what about *Huck Finn*?

VIEWPOINT

"While the First Amendment guarantees freedom of speech . . . it does not obligate the government to fund artists (or museums) taking advantage of free speech rights."

Government Should Not Fund Controversial Art

Joseph Perkins

Many artists and museums rely on public grants as a means of support. In the following viewpoint, Joseph Perkins discusses a controversial art exhibit sponsored by the Brooklyn, New York, Museum of Art in late 1999. Perkins contends that some of the art on display is obscene and the American public should not be forced to support obscenity with their tax dollars. He asserts that artists and museums should be subsidized by the private sector, not by the government. Perkins is an editorial writer for the *San Diego Union-Tribune*.

As you read, consider the following questions:
1. According to Perkins, why is Chris Ofili's painting, *The Holy Virgin Mary*, so controversial?
2. What happened in Cincinnati when a museum displayed photographs by Robert Mapplethorpe?

Reprinted, with permission, from "Why Must We Pay for Insults Masquerading as Art?" by Joseph Perkins, *The San Diego Union-Tribune*, October 1, 1999.

C hris Ofili must be pleased as punch. He's the British "artist" whose highly offensive painting, "The Holy Virgin Mary," has ignited a political and cultural firestorm in New York City.

With no concern whatsoever for the sensibilities of New York's Catholic community, the Brooklyn Museum of Art fully intends to display the artist's controversial piece—a portrait of the Holy Mother adorned with elephant dung and surrounded by pictures of buttocks (call it mixed media)—when it opens a new exhibit.

The museum's board of directors is all the more determined to stand behind Ofili's work in the wake of threats by New York Mayor Rudy Guiliani to withdraw the $7 million the museum receives from the city out of its $23 million annual budget.

So the museum has gone to court accusing the mayor of trampling upon the First Amendment. Guiliani's threat to withdraw city funding unless "Virgin Mary" is crated back to England is nothing less than government censorship, they sneer.

The New York art dispute brings to mind similar art-related flaps that have made the national news over the past decade.

A half-dozen years ago, it may be recalled, a San Diego trio, David Avalos, Louis Hock and Elizabeth Sisco, thought they would make an artistic statement about immigration by taking federal grant money they received from the National Endowment for the Arts and passing it out, in $10 bills, to illegal aliens.

The aim of this "conceptual art piece," which they entitled "Arte-Reembolso/Art Rebate," was to redefine public art, they explained, using symbolism, gesture and performance.

Three years before the taxpayer-bankrolled "Art Rebate," the NEA had gotten into trouble for subsidizing the "art" of Andres Serrano, whose most noteworthy piece was a photograph of a plastic crucifix in a beaker of urine, which he cleverly entitled "Piss Christ."

When the hoi polloi expressed indignation, Serrano pompously responded, "As an artist, I stand my ground."

Then there was the infamous exhibit of so-called "homoerotic" art by the late Robert Mapplethorpe, which toured the country at the beginning of the decade. Among other works included in the taxpayer-subsidized exhibit was a photograph of a man with a bullwhip inserted in his derriere (not to mention pictures of children in erotic poses).

The Mapplethorpe exhibit was so provocative, in fact, that a Cincinnati judge actually ordered a local museum curator to stand trial on misdemeanor obscenity charges for publicly displaying pornography under the guise of "art."

Defenders of Mapplethorpe, of Serrano, of Avalos, Hock and Sisco, and, now, of Ofili, hide behind the First Amendment, arguing that no matter how offensive an artwork may be to a certain segment of a given community, it enjoys constitutional protection.

FREEDOM OF POINTLESS EXPRESSION

Reprinted with permission of Kirk Anderson.

However, while the First Amendment guarantees freedom of speech—and let us accept that "art," in all its permutations, amounts to "speech"—it does not obligate the government to fund artists (or museums) taking advantage of free speech rights.

Indeed, the Brooklyn Museum of Art has every prerogative to exhibit Ofili's dung-stained painting—the Catholic community and opinion writers be damned—but the museum's directors have no right to expect taxpayers to subsidize work they find patently offensive.

And one needn't be Catholic to find Ofili's painting offensive. The art elite may consider it some kind of contemporary masterpiece. But when you really get down to it, it's simply a hate crime masquerading as art.

Indeed, it's no different than a spray painted swastika on a Jewish synagogue (which could be called a mural). No different than a cross set ablaze on the lawn of a black church (which could be described as conceptual sculpture, with found objects).

Consider the absurdity of asking the Jewish community to subsidize the spray paint used to desecrate a synagogue or the black community to help pay for the lighter fluid used to burn a cross in front of one its churches.

Well it's no less absurd to ask Catholics (as well as offended non-Catholics) to blithely accept the expenditure of their tax dollars on art that disparages a sacred religious figure.

That's why the government ought to get out of the business of funding artists, either directly or indirectly.

If there is an audience for such offending "artists" as Avalos, Hock and Sisco, and Serrano and Mapplethorpe and, yes, Ofili, let that audience subsidize their work—by writing checks to museums or other arts organizations—rather than relying on the entire taxpaying public to do so.

"The proposed withdrawal of public sector aid to the arts . . . would have wide economic and cultural repercussions at the state and grass roots levels."

Government Funding of the Arts Is Necessary

Harold Jaffe

Debates over controversial art typically examine whether the public—through the National Endowment for the Arts—should subsidize art that some people find offensive. In the following viewpoint, Harold Jaffe contends that the amount of public funds subsidizing the arts is miniscule compared to the returns generated by the art industry. He maintains that forcing artists and museums to rely solely on the private sector for support instead of government funds would result in bland, boring art that would not challenge the boundaries of convention. In addition, support from agencies such as the NEA and National Endowment for the Humanities has allowed the number of state art councils, orchestras, and dance, theater and opera companies to increase and flourish. Jaffe, an English professor at San Diego State University, has received two grants for fiction writing from the National Endowment for the Arts.

As you read, consider the following questions:

1. How much does the individual American taxpayer contribute each year to support the arts, according to Jaffe?
2. In Jaffe's opinion, why is it acceptable if some artists offend and grandstand with their art?

Reprinted, with permission, from "Art, Mortality, and American Politics," by Harold Jaffe, *The San Diego Union-Tribune*, October 6, 1999.

It's as predictable as flu season: a contemporary art exhibition hits town headlining "controversial" art, and politicians looking to advertise their virtue become offended and make denunciations in the name of morality. In this instance it is the Brooklyn Museum of Art's exhibition: "Sensation: Young British Artists from the Saatchi Collection."

New York City Mayor Rudolph Giuliani, battling Hillary Clinton for a Senate seat and evidently desperate for any sure-fire issue to bolster his popularity, has labeled the exhibition "sick stuff" and ordered the Brooklyn Museum to cancel it. When the museum refused, Giuliani froze $7 million in operating funds and began eviction proceedings. The Brooklyn Museum, which is 176 years old and has occupied its current site for a century, receives $7 million a year from the city in monthly installments of $500,000.

Instead of knuckling under, the museum has filed a federal lawsuit against the mayor for violating its First Amendment rights as well as its constitutionally guaranteed equal rights under the law.

Highlighting the several works the mayor denounced is a "blasphemous" painting by Chris Ofili entitled "The Holy Virgin Mary," in which a representation of the Virgin, in black, is splattered with elephant dung. The image, ironically combining a religious icon and animal waste, recalls Andres Serrano's notorious "Piss Christ," which, 10 years ago, provoked Sen. Jesse Helms' wrath, and which subsequently led to the partial dismantling of the National Endowment for the Arts.

Helms' response then, like Giuliani's now, is to let those purveyors of filth-masked-as-art find their own subsidization. But don't expect the taxpayer to contribute one cent of his or her hard-earned money in support.

The Economics of Art

Rather than debate the artistic merits of "The Holy Virgin Mary," or the parameters of contemporary art, let me cite the following: The individual American taxpayer contributes about 65 cents a year to support the arts, which is 50 times lower than that of major industrial nations such as Canada, Germany, the Netherlands, Japan, France or the United

Kingdom. Berlin itself spends more on federal aid to art annually than does the entire United States.

As far as privatizing all support to the arts, which is what Helms and Giuliani want, what would that mean practically? Applying to Microsoft to fund art which interrogates the values contributing to the ascendancy of corporations such as Microsoft? Artists would be forced to follow the corporate line or perish through lack of support. Not much different in principle from Soviet party-line art during the Stalin era.

Wiley Miller/*San Francisco Examiner*. Reprinted by permission.

Moreover, the large picture indicates that the arts actually earn more than they cost. According to the National Assembly of Local Arts Agencies, the arts nationwide constitute a "$37 billion industry employing 1.3 million people, or 1.5 percent of the work force, and generating tax revenues of $3.4 billion." Rather than "subsisting primarily on charity," the nonprofit arts industry "actually generates 60 percent of its budget with cash sales" and has a measurable, positive impact on the federal, state and local treasuries.

The proposed withdrawal of public sector aid to the arts, then, would have wide economic and cultural repercussions at the state and grass roots levels. As the New York-based Literary Network points out, "Before the creation of the National Endowment for the Arts in 1965, only five states had state-funded arts councils. Today, all 50 states do."

Through the efforts of the NEA and NEH (National Endowment for the Humanities) over the last 34 years, the "number of state orchestras has increased from 110 to 230; nonprofit theater companies from 56 to 425; dance companies from 37 to 450; and opera companies from 27 to 120."

Are the American people prepared to demolish the cultural infrastructure of our country? If the New Yorkers' outpouring of support for the Brooklyn Museum and denunciation of Giuliani's "cultural terrorism" is any index, Americans will reject demagoguery in the guise of civic virtue.

The point has been made innumerable times: We're a complex and multifarious nation. This fact is trumpeted when the United States wants to make a statement about the uniqueness of its democracy.

Art and Democracy

But how can a nation remain truly democratic, which is to say, deeply integrated, without its imaginative consciences: its artists? Not artists in service to the state, or to Microsoft or Nike, but committed to the prerogatives of their imaginations.

Of course some artists will overstate and offend and grandstand. But that is what art-making is about: trial and error, taking imaginative risks and failing twice or half-a-dozen times before succeeding admirably. Think of Walt Whitman, Zora Neale Hurston, Jackson Pollock, Andy Warhol, Frank Zappa, Jim Morrison, Janice Joplin, Allen Ginsberg, all to one extent or another considered renegades in their time, but now proudly institutionalized in our culture.

As one of the readers of the Sensation exhibition catalogue put it in his response on Amazon.com: "If you don't like it, relax. It's only art. It can't bite you."

Periodical Bibliography

The following articles have been selected to supplement the diverse views presented in this chapter. Addresses are provided for periodicals not indexed in the *Readers' Guide to Periodical Literature*, the *Alternative Press Index*, the *Social Sciences Index*, or the *Index to Legal Periodicals and Books.*

Linda Chavez	"Where Is Tipper When We Really Need Her?" *George*, September 2000. Available from PO Box 50192, Boulder, CO 80322.
Jim D'Entremont	"The Devil's Disciples," *Index on Censorship*, November/ December 1998.
John Garvey	"'Sensation' in Brooklyn," *Commonweal*, November 19, 1999.
Walter Gibbs	"In Norway, a Nanny Standard for Movies," *The New York Times*, July 8, 1999.
Charles Gordon	"Much Ado About Violence," *Maclean's*, May 24, 1999.
Bob Herbert	"A Chill Grows in Brooklyn," *The New York Times*, September 27, 1999.
John Leo	"Hello, Dung Lovers," *U.S. News & World Report*, October 11, 1999.
John Leo	"Hold the Chocolate," *U.S. News & World Report*, July 13, 1998.
Joseph I. Lieberman and John McCain	"The No-Show Summit," *The New York Times*, May 12, 1999.
Steven Henry Madoff	"Shock for Shock's Sake?" *Time*, October 11, 1999.
Marcia Pally	"'Decency' in the Arts," *Tikkun*, November/ December 1998.
Katha Pollitt	"Catholic Bashing?" *Nation*, November 1, 1999.
Virginia Postrel	"When Movies Become 'Product,'" *The New York Times*, June 14, 1999.
Margaret O'Brien Steinfels	"Artists Have Rights, and So Do Taxpayers," *The New York Times*, September 25, 1999.
George F. Will	"The Art of Funding," *Newsweek*, July 6, 1998.
George Wilson	"Furor over Painting Reveals Conflicted Attitudes Towards the Body, Sexuality," *National Catholic Reporter*, December 10, 1999. Available from PO Box 473, Mount Morris, IL 61054-0473.

For Further Discussion

Chapter 1

1. If you agree that censorship is necessary, consider the following questions: If the government were to begin censoring the media, who should be the censors? Should there be a national censor, or a censor for each state, or for each community, or for each type of media (for example, newspapers, magazines, movies, music, Internet)? Should the censors be appointed or elected, and how long should they serve? What should the censors do after their terms are over, since they have been exposed to many ideas other Americans were not allowed to see?

2. Richard Curtis argues that the Nuremberg Files—a website that listed the names, addresses, and phone numbers of abortion providers, as well as their children's names and schools they attended—threatened doctors and their staffs and was therefore not protected by the right to free speech. Robyn Blumner contends that the website did not violate the right to free speech because no explicit threats were made to any of the people whose names were on the list. Based on your reading of the viewpoints, should the Nuremberg Files website have been protected by the First Amendment? Why or why not?

3. Burning the American flag sends a definite message, yet supporters of a constitutional amendment to ban flag desecration argue that the amendment will not violate the right to free speech because flag burning is conduct, not speech. Do you agree? Why or why not? Would an amendment against flag desecration stop people from burning flags in protest, or would it lead to more people burning flags? Explain your answer.

4. The U.S. Supreme Court ruled in *Texas v. Johnson* in 1989 that burning a flag is political speech and therefore it is protected by the First Amendment. Justice William Brennan wrote, "Our tolerance of criticism . . . is a sign and source of our strength." Explain what this means.

Chapter 2

1. Robert H. Bork argues that America has become a pornographic culture since standards regulating the censorship of pornography have relaxed. Do you agree with his assessment that America's moral decline is due to the influx of sexually explicit material? Why or why not?

2. Dan Coats and Charles Levendosky debate the constitutionality and effectiveness of laws regulating pornography on the Internet. Which argument is strongest? Support your answer using examples from the viewpoints.

3. Bruce Watson believes that creating a separate domain for pornographic sites on the Internet will protect minors from sexually explicit material online. Do you agree, or will a domain for adult sites attract children who are looking for pornographic sites? Explain. Would it be a violation of the First Amendment to require these pornographic sites to use a separate domain, as Jon Weinberg contends? Why or why not?

Chapter 3

1. Helen Chaffee Biehle contends that if children must be eighteen years old to buy a book or CD in a store, then they should have to be eighteen to check the same materials out from a library. Do you agree? Why or why not? Should libraries inform parents if their children check out material that some may consider offensive? Should libraries purchase these books or CDs in the first place? Who should decide what may be offensive and what is not? Explain your answers.

2. Kathleen Parker argues that children under eighteen should use computers equipped with filtering software at the library to prevent them from being exposed to pornographic material. The Intellectual Freedom Committee of the American Library Association argues against computer software filters, claiming that the filters are a form of censorship that sometimes blocks access to materials the filters are not designed to block. Which argument is strongest? Support your answer with examples from the viewpoints.

Chapter 4

1. David Lowenthal argues that explicit scenes of sex and violence portrayed in movies, television, and music have directly contributed to the decline of American society, and therefore, the entertainment industry should be censored to protect social values. Virginia Postrel argues that such censorship standards are too arbitrary to permit because people differ in their views of what constitutes excessive violence. Which argument is stronger? Explain your answer.

2. Joseph Perkins describes several examples of controversial "art" that have received taxpayer funding over the years. In your opinion, are his examples "art" or are they obscenities? Can something be offensive and still be art? Explain your answers.

3. Harold Jaffe argues that because the amount individual taxpayers contribute to publicly funded art is so little and the return is so large, government funding of the arts is necessary for economic and cultural reasons. Do you agree with his contention? Does the fact that Jaffe is the recipient of two grants from the National Endowment for the Arts affect your assessment of his argument? Why or why not?

Organizations to Contact

The editors have compiled the following list of organizations concerned with issues debated in this book. The descriptions are derived from materials provided by the organizations. All have publications or information available for interested readers. The list was compiled on the date of publication of the present volume; the information provided here may change. Be aware that many organizations take several weeks or longer to respond to inquiries, so allow as much time as possible.

American Civil Liberties Union (ACLU)
125 Broad St., 18th Floor, New York, NY 10004
(212) 549-2500 • fax: (212) 549-2646
e-mail: aclu@aclu.org • website: www.aclu.org

The ACLU is a national organization that defends Americans' civil rights guaranteed in the U.S. Constitution. It adamantly opposes regulation of all forms of speech, including pornography and hate speech. The ACLU offers numerous reports, fact sheets, and policy statements on a wide variety of issues. Publications include the briefing papers "Freedom of Expression," "Hate Speech on Campus," and "Popular Music Under Siege."

American Library Association (ALA)
50 E. Huron St., Chicago, IL 60611
(800) 545-2433 • fax: (312) 440-9374
e-mail: ala@ala.org • website: www.ala.org

The ALA is the nation's primary professional organization for librarians. Through its Office for Intellectual Freedom (OIF), the ALA supports free access to libraries and library materials. The OIF also monitors and opposes efforts to ban books. The ALA's sister organization, the Freedom to Read Foundation, provides legal defense for libraries. Publications include the *Newsletter on Intellectual Freedom*, articles, fact sheets, and policy statements, including "Protecting the Freedom to Read."

Canadian Association for Free Expression (CAFE)
PO Box 332, Station B, Etobicoke, ON M9W 5L3 Canada
(905) 897-7221
e-mail: cafe@canadafirst.net
website: www.canadianfreespeech.com

CAFE, one of Canada's leading civil liberties groups, works to strengthen the freedom of speech and freedom of expression provisions in the Canadian Charter of Rights and Freedoms. It lobbies politicians and researches threats to freedom of speech. Publications include specialized reports, leaflets, and *The Free Speech Monitor*, which is published ten times per year.

Concerned Women for America (CWA)
1015 Fifteenth St. NW, Suite 1100, Washington, DC 20005
(202) 488-7000 • fax: (202) 488-0806
website: www.cwfa.org

CWA is a membership organization that promotes conservative values and is concerned with creating an environment that is conducive to building strong families and raising healthy children. CWA publishes the monthly *Family Voice*, which argues against all forms of pornography.

Electronic Frontier Foundation (EFF)
1550 Bryant St., Suite 725, San Francisco, CA 94103-4832
(415) 436-9333 • fax: (415) 436-9993
e-mail: ask@eff.org • website: www.eff.org

EFF is a nonprofit, nonpartisan organization that works to protect privacy and freedom of expression in the arena of computers and the Internet. Its missions include supporting litigation that protects First Amendment rights. EFF's website publishes an electronic bulletin, *Effector*, and the guidebook *Protecting Yourself Online: The Definitive Resource on Safety, Freedom, and Privacy in Cyberspace*.

Family Research Council (FRC)
700 13th St. NW, Suite 500, Washington, DC 20005
(202) 393-2100 • fax: (202) 393-2134
e-mail: corrdept@frc.org • website: www.frc.org

The Family Research Council is an organization that believes pornography degrades women and children and seeks to strengthen current obscenity laws. It publishes the monthly newsletter *Washington Watch* and the bimonthly journal *Family Policy*, which features a full-length essay in each issue, such as "Keeping Libraries User and Family Friendly: The Challenge of Internet Pornography." The FRC also publishes policy papers, including "Indecent Proposal: The NEA Since the Supreme Court Decency Decision," and "Internet Filtering and Blocking Technology."

Freedom Forum
1101 Wilson Blvd., Arlington, VA 22209
(703) 528-0800 • (703) 284-2836
e-mail: news@freedomforum.org • website: www.freedomforum.org

The Freedom Forum is an international organization that works to protect freedom of the press and free speech. It monitors developments in media and First Amendment issues on its website, in its monthly magazine *Forum News*, and in the *Media Studies Journal*, published twice a year.

Free Speech Coalition
PO Box 10480, Canoga Park, CA 91309
(800) 845-8503 or (818) 348-9373
e-mail freespeech@pacificnet.net • www.freespeechcoalition.com

The coalition is a trade association that represents members of the adult entertainment industry. It seeks to protect the industry from attempts to censor pornography. Publications include fact sheets, *Free Speech X-Press*, and the report *The Truth About the Adult Entertainment Industry*.

International Freedom of Expression Exchange (IFEX)
IFEX Clearing House
489 College St., Suite 403, Toronto, ON M6G 1A5 Canada
(416) 515-9622 • fax: (416) 515-7879
e-mail: ifex@ifex.org • website: www.ifex.org

IFEX consists of more than forty organizations that support the freedom of expression. Its work is coordinated by the Toronto-based Clearing House. Through the Action Alert Network, organizations report abuses of free expression to the Clearing House, which distributes that information throughout the world. Publications include the weekly *The Communiqué*, which reports on free expression triumphs and violations.

Morality in Media (MIM)
475 Riverside Dr., Suite 239, New York, NY 10115
(212) 870-3222 • fax: (212) 870-2765
e-mail: mim@moralityinmedia.org
website: www.moralityinmedia.org

Morality in Media is an interfaith organization that fights obscenity and opposes indecency in the mainstream media. It believes pornography harms society and maintains the National Obscenity Law Center, a clearinghouse of legal materials on obscenity law. Publications include the bimonthlies *Morality in Media* and *Obscenity Law Bulletin* and reports, including "Pornography's Effects on Adults and Children."

National Coalition Against Censorship (NCAC)
275 Seventh Ave., New York, NY 10001
(212) 807-6222 • fax: (212) 807-6245
e-mail: ncac@ncac.org • website: www.ncac.org
The coalition represents more than forty national organizations that work to prevent suppression of free speech and the press. NCAC educates the public about the dangers of censorship and how to oppose it. The coalition publishes *Censorship News* five times a year, articles, various reports, and background papers. Papers include "Censorship's Tools Du Jour: V-Chips, TV Ratings, PICS, and Internet Filters."

National Coalition for the Protection of Children & Families
800 Compton Rd., Suite 9224, Cincinnati, OH 45231-9964
(513) 521-6227 • fax: (513) 521-6337
website: www.nationalcoalition.org
The coalition is an organization of business, religious, and civic leaders who work to eliminate pornography. It encourages citizens to support the enforcement of obscenity laws and to close down neighborhood pornography outlets. Publications include the books *Final Report of the Attorney General's Commission on Pornography*, *The Mind Polluters*, and *Pornography: A Human Tragedy*.

People for the American Way (PFAW)
2000 M St. NW, Suite 400, Washington, DC 20036
(202) 467-4999 or 1-800-326-PFAW • fax: (202) 293-2672
e-mail: pfaw@pfaw.org • website: www.pfaw.org
PFAW works to promote citizen participation in democracy and safeguard the principles of the U.S. Constitution, including the right to free speech. It publishes a variety of fact sheets, articles, and position statements on its website and distributes the e-mail newsletter *Freedom to Learn Online*.

Bibliography of Books

Robert H. Bork

Slouching Towards Gomorrah: Modern Liberalism and American Decline. New York: Regan Books, 1996.

June Edwards

Opposing Censorship in Public Schools: Religion, Morality, and Literature. Mahwah, NJ: Lawrence Erlbaum Associates, 1998.

Owen M. Fiss

The Irony of Free Speech. Cambridge, MA: Harvard University Press, 1996.

Mike Godwin

Cyber Rights: Defending Free Speech in the Digital Age. New York: Random House, 1998.

Mary E. Hull

Censorship in America: A Reference Handbook. Santa Barbara, CA: ABC-CLIO, 1999.

Peter Irons, ed.

May It Please the Court: The First Amendment: Transcripts of the Oral Arguments Made Before the Supreme Court in Sixteen Key First Amendment Cases. New York: New Press, 1997.

Alan Charles Kors and Harvey A. Silverglate

The Shadow University: The Betrayal of Liberty on America's Campuses. New York: Free Press, 1998.

Laura Lederer and Richard Delgado, eds.

The Price We Pay: The Case Against Racist Speech, Hate Propaganda, and Pornography. New York: Hill and Wang, 1995.

Laurence R. Marcus

Fighting Words: The Politics of Hateful Speech. Westport, CT: Praeger, 1996.

Gail Blasser Riley

Censorship. New York: Facts On File, 1998.

Timothy C. Shiell

Campus Hate Speech on Trial. Lawrence: University Press of Kansas, 1998.

Rod Smolla

Deliberate Intent: A Lawyer Tells the True Story of Murder by the Book. New York: Crown, 1999.

Jonathan Wallace and Mark Mangan

Sex, Laws, and Cyberspace: Freedom and Regulation on the Frontiers of the Online Revolution. New York: Henry Holt, 1996.

Frank Walsh

Sin and Censorship: The Catholic Church and the Motion Picture Industry. New Haven, CT: Yale University Press, 1996.

Mark I. West

Trust Your Children: Voices Against Censorship in Children's Literature. New York: Neal-Schuman, 1997.

Nicholas Wolfson

Hate Speech, Sex Speech, Free Speech. Westport, CT: Praeger, 1997.

Index

185